Active Learning for Infants

Debby Cryer

Thelma Harms

Beth Bourland

Frank Porter Graham Child Development Center
University of North Carolina, Chapel Hill, North Carolina

Addison-Wesley Publishing Company
Menlo Park, California • Reading, Massachusetts • Don Mills, Ontario
Wokingham, England • Amsterdam • Sydney • Singapore
Tokyo • Madrid • Bogotá • Santiago • San Juan

This book is published by Addison Wesley Longman, Inc.

Developed with the partial support of the North Carolina Department of Human Resources, Office of Day Care Services, with funds provided by the Social Services Block Grant.

Design: Paula Shuhert
Cover Design: Lydia D'moch
Illustrations: Cynthia Swann Brodie
            Jane McCreary

ISBN 0-201-21334-6
15 16-DR-00 99

Acknowledgments

*T*hese materials for infants could not have been developed without the time and talent of a large number of day care and materials production professionals.

Funding for the project originated from the Office of Day Care Services, North Carolina Department of Human Resources, directed by Rachel Fesmire. Continuous contact with this agency was provided through the very supportive project officer, Beth May, whose careful and timely reviews of the materials were sincerely appreciated.

The Advisory Board, listed below, was a hard-working, knowledgeable group that reviewed all the materials and offered excellent suggestions. Those members who had access to groups of infants also helped us try out the activities.

Peggy Ball
Program Coordinator for Occupational
    Service
Dept. of Community Colleges
Raleigh

Sue Baynes
Baynes Happy Day Nursery and
    Kindergarten, Inc.
Greensboro

Frances Britton
Director of Day Care Division
United Day Care Services
Greensboro

Helen Canaday
School of Home Economics
University of North Carolina
Greensboro

Dennis Ferguson
Supervisor of Planning and Reporting
    Unit
Office of Day Care Services
Raleigh

Jane Hall
Asst. Professor
Western Carolina University
Cullowhee

Sylvia Hall
Owner, Winterpark Preschool
Wilmington

Terry Jarvis
Infant/Toddler Teacher
Charlotte

Beth May
Supervisor, Training and Technical
    Assistance Unit
Office of Day Care Services
Raleigh

Juliette McKoy
Licensing Consultant
Raleigh

Alfreida Parker
Day Care Specialist
Office of Day Care Services
Greenville

Holly Willett
Bush Fellow
Frank Porter Graham Child
    Development Center
Chapel Hill

Pilot testing of the activities with groups of infants was done by teacher and directors in 17 North Carolina centers. Their feedback assured us that the activities do work in the real world of day care.

Busy Bee Day Care Center
Aurora
Jane Brooks, Director

Robin's Nest
Robbinsville
Carol Orr, Director

Better Beginnings, Inc.
Kitty Hawk
Charlotte Walker, Director

St. John's Learning Center
Waynesville
Jackie Spencer, Director

Miss Nancy's Nursery
Morehead City
Nancy Pollock, Director

Cullowhee Child Development Center
Cullowhee
Cathy Arps, Director

Method Day Care Center
Raleigh
Dorothy Wilson, Director

First Presbyterian Child Care Center
Durham
Kathy Gillespie, Director

Worthdale Child Development Center
Raleigh
Hope Drayton, Director

Tiny Tots
Hillsborough
Carolyn Roberts, Director

Hathaway's Hunny Tree, Inc.
Tarboro
Joyce Hathaway, Director

Bi-City Center for Children and Youth
Chapel Hill
Patsy Barbee, Director

Church Street Child Development Center
Black Mountain
Dorothy Styles, Director

Pitt Community College Preschool Lab
Greenville
Sue Creech, Director

Groce Preschool Center
Asheville
Nancy Kirchner, Director

Developmental Day Care
High Point
Louise Neth, Director

Pilot Baptist Day Care Center
Zebulon
Jo Brewster and Kim Denton, Directors

Norma Locke, project secretary, developed an ingenious method for using the word processor to print out the activities within the original page design, which made the enormous task of materials preparation possible. She was assisted by Ruth Brown and Charlsena Stone.

Subsequent training conducted by the authors for Navy Child Care Center Directors in the use of these activities resulted in the development of additional caregiver training materials. We appreciate the support and encouragement given by the Navy Child Care Coordinator, Carolee Callen, and Assistant Coordinator, Barbara Nophlin.

We are most grateful to everyone who contributed knowledge, energy, and enthusiasm to this project.

Contents

Activities for Learning from the World Around Them

Planning for Infants

Quality Care for Infants

Caregivers of infants are special people. They play a very big part today in helping parents raise babies. Babies learn and grow best when they get high quality care. This book will make it easier for you to give *quality* care to your babies.

There has been a lot of talk about the difference between "custodial care" and "developmental care." Custodial care is routine care that pays attention only to the baby's basic needs, such as being fed, changed, and kept clean and safe. Developmental care does all those things, as well as taking care of the baby's needs to be held, loved, and talked to; to be given things to look at and listen to; to play outside of the crib and be given help to do more things on his own.

Quality care is care that helps children develop both their minds and bodies in a safe and healthy place. Providing quality care is not an easy job. That's why caregivers of infants have to make everything they do count for developmental care.

The activities in this book are short and easy to do. Many of them can be done while taking care of basic needs, such as feeding and diaper changing. The key is to remember that babies are learning from the very start. Caregivers play a very important part in what babies learn.

The Active Learning Series

The Active Learning Series is made up of activity books for infants, one-, two-, and three-year-olds. In each of these books there is a planning guide and four activity sections. *Active Learning for Infants* has many ideas for children with abilities up to 12 months of age. This book includes the following sections.

Planning For Infants

This section has ideas for setting up your space and schedule to provide good care and avoid problems. It includes ways to handle infants so that there is a time and place for activities. It shows how to plan so that infant care goes smoothly.

Activities for Listening and Talking

This section has ideas to help you make the best use of talking to infants all through the day. It also has play ideas using books, pictures, and puppets. Activities are numbered 1 through 48.

Activities for Physical Development

This section has ideas to develop the large muscles, such as those in the legs, arms, and back. It also has ideas to develop the small muscles in the hands and fingers to help babies grasp, hold, and pick things up. Activities are numbered 49 through 120.

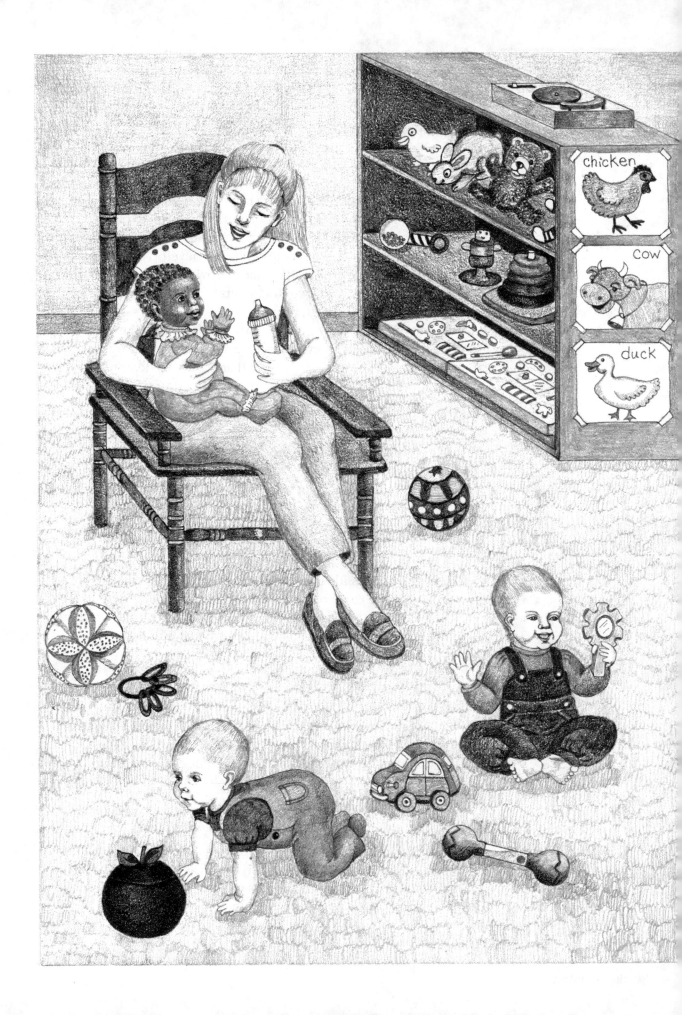

> ### *Creative Activities*
>
> This section has activities with art, blocks, dramatic play, and music. These ideas help to develop the senses, the imagination, and the skills to enjoy the arts. Activities are numbered 121 through 228.

> ### *Activities for Learning from the World Around Them*
>
> This section has activities using nature, the senses, size, shape, color, and numbers. These help babies enjoy and learn about the world around them. Activities are numbered 229 through 345.

Sharing Ideas with Parents

Parents are interested in what you do for their children. It makes parents feel good to know that you have been doing special things just for their baby. Share the ideas in this book with parents.

- Tell parents about an activity their baby likes.
- Have some things in your room for parents to borrow and read. Cut out articles from magazines and put them in folders. Let parents know that you have these materials that they can borrow.
- Call state offices and agencies for free materials on child care topics. They may have materials on feeding children, growth of children, or ways parents can spot problems.
- Have a meeting for parents where you show a film or slides and talk about helpful ideas for raising children. Feeding baby or handling typical baby problems such as crying or separating from parents are good topics to start with. Your local community college or Agricultural Extension Agent may be able to help with speakers, films, or other resources.
- Keep a bulletin board near the entrance with current information about center activities, notices about parenting education, and fun things to do with children.
- Give parents information daily on the things their children do. Help the parents follow the baby's schedule by telling them what the child ate, when the child napped, and how the child played each day.

Helping Babies Feel Special

Babies need to know that you really care about them. They know this from your kind tone of voice and gentle touch. They feel good when you look into their eyes as you talk to them and meet their needs rapidly. Babies are unhappy when you handle them in a rough or unfriendly way, use a loud voice, or ignore them when they cry. The way you relate to the babies in your care is very important. It helps shape the way a child sees himself.

Developmental care means that you show children you value and like them. Throughout this book, you will find ideas to help baby feel special. Although there are no separate activities for social and emotional growth, emotional support is part of all the activities. Be sure to follow these ideas to help babies feel good about themselves.

- Look right into baby's eyes when you talk. It helps her feel important and special.
- Use baby's name when you talk to him. It makes what you say more personal.

- Use a kind tone of voice and gentle touch. Hold and cuddle baby often. It shows you care.
- Use routines as a time to talk to and work with infants. It gives them special attention while they get personal care.
- React to what babies do with praise and delight. It helps them feel happy with what they do.
- Have conversations with baby by repeating her sounds back to her. It shows her that you are listening.
- Talk to babies often. It builds a happy relationship.

Handling Problems

Babies up to one year old are usually a joy to care for. They haven't really learned to say "no" yet. They don't fight with each other. For many months they don't move around much, so it's easy to keep them safe. They are cuddly, can be amused by the most unexciting things, and nothing is nicer than a baby's toothless smile or brand new laugh.

But once in a while every baby will be hard to deal with. Some babies find things in life more upsetting than others do, and they don't keep that a secret.

Crying is the main problem an infant caregiver has to deal with. It's the baby's way of letting you know that something is wrong. Studies have been done on babies to find out which babies cry more, those who are allowed to cry or those whose cries are answered quickly. It turns out that babies who are answered quickly cry *less* than those who have to cry a long time before they get what they need. The quickly answered babies are happier because they have learned that adults will love, help, and care for them. They are less anxious and grow up to be happier and more independent. In some cases, babies have given up on crying and don't cry at all because they are rarely answered. These children usually grow up without being able to trust in others and have many problems throughout life.

These studies have shown us how important it is to answer babies quickly whenever they cry. This can be difficult for you when you care for a group of infants. Here are some tips to help you help babies cry less.

- Answer baby's cries as quickly as you can. It helps baby learn to trust you. Soon he will cry less and wait patiently because he knows you will help as soon as you can.
- Stay calm when working with babies. They will cry less when they know things are going well and that you are not anxious or upset.
- Let babies adjust to new people or situations in their own time. Slowly help each child to learn to accept and enjoy new things. Babies in a new place or with new people need to be held more.

- Get to know each baby well. Learn the different things that soothe or upset each baby.
- If baby's routine care needs are met and baby is still crying, try to figure out why. Ask yourself questions like these: Is baby bored? Does she need to get away from too much action? Is he feeling well? Does she need extra cuddling today? Is he bothered by another child? If holding or cuddling helps, make sure baby gets plenty.
- Babies should not be left to cry it out. If a baby cries for more than three minutes before going to sleep, check to see what you can do to make her feel more relaxed and secure.

Helping Baby Say Good-bye

All babies have a hard time saying good-bye to their parents at one time or another. This is part of learning to love. It's common for babies who are six to 12 months old to have a harder time with this than at other ages, although many children have problems earlier or later, too.

Here are some ways to make saying good-bye easier for baby.

- Help parents feel at ease about leaving their baby with you. Invite them in to see how you care for children. Answer all their questions freely. Tell them they are welcome any time they want to visit. Babies know when their parents are worried, so work hard to make parents feel secure.
- Show baby how happy you are to have her with you. Give her lots of attention when she arrives. Help her settle into the day.
- Be ready for baby to have problems in settling down if he has been away for a while. It will take time for him to remember you and get used to the way you do things.
- Be sympathetic to a baby who has trouble saying good-bye. Remember how hard it is for you to say good-bye to someone you love. It's harder for babies because they don't really understand that the person they love will come back.
- Keep some familiar things around so baby will feel more at home — a favorite blanket, a doll or a stuffed animal baby knows.

Helping Baby Give Up the Bottle in the Crib

All of us know that bottles in the crib are not good for babies. Milk or juice stays too long in baby's mouth and can cause tooth decay. Ear infections can also be caused by giving baby the bottle while he's lying down. But many babies cry and won't go to sleep without a bottle. Here are a few ideas for helping baby give up the bottle in the crib.

- Feed baby only while you hold her. Do not ever prop a bottle or feed baby in her crib.

- Feed each baby on his own schedule. Then you won't have to feed everyone at the same time.
- Try feeding baby until she's asleep in your arms. Then gently put her into her crib for her nap.
- If feeding baby to sleep in your arms doesn't work, try a pacifier in the crib. Pat baby's back and sing gentle songs.
- Don't force baby to adjust too quickly. Let him give up the bottle in the crib with lots of help from you.
- Work with baby's parents. If they have problems getting baby to sleep without the bottle, suggest that they use only water in the crib bottle. This will help save baby's teeth.

Making Time for Activities in the Schedule

The way you use the time babies spend with you is called *the schedule.* Everything that is done for care and play needs its own time in the schedule. You must make time for both care and play.

When you are gone and someone else is taking care of the babies, he or she will need to know the schedule. If you write down the main things you do and when you do them, then others who care for the babies can do things at the same time.

Any schedule set up for infants has to be flexible. This is because each baby seems to live by his own clock. Try to keep the babies on their home schedules. Then you won't have to feed or diaper all the babies at the same time. Check diapers as you carry babies from one activity to another. Write down when you change diapers so that you will get some idea about times for the next day. This information can help parents, too. Make washing your hands after diapering and cleaning the diapering area part of your routine, so that you will wash up without having to think about it.

It helps if one caregiver takes care of a small group of infants. In a room where there is more than one caregiver, the whole group of infants should be split and a small group given to each adult. This does not mean that caregivers should not cooperate with each other or use the same space. But it does mean that one person is responsible for being sure the needs of a smaller group of babies are met. Care by the same person helps the child form a bond with the caregiver. This also helps the caregiver get to know the babies and make up better schedules for them.

Use routine care, such as diapering and feeding, as a time to give a baby personal attention. With a little planning, many of the activities in this book can be done during routine care times and will not add much work for you. During routine care, talk to babies, look at mobiles or pictures hung near the care area, and sing songs. As you plan the activities make sure to choose some that can be done during routine care.

Activity Tips

Plan activities *ahead* of time.

- Choose activities that match a baby's skills.
- Go over the instructions for the activities you have chosen.
- Get together the things that you will need.
- Write your plans on a planning form.
- Plan for both morning and afternoon play.

Decide where you will do each activity.

- Cribs should be for sleeping, not for activities. Awake time needs to be spent out of the crib.
- Set up an open play area for the smaller babies with infant seats, a blanket, a rod and hook to hang toys, and open shelves. This lets you have many things going on all around the room.
- Separate the babies who don't move around from the crawling and walking babies during play times when you can't be right next to the children.
- Put babies on blankets or soft rugs on the floor.
- Use infant seats or boxes with pillows to prop baby.
- Try infant swings and walkers.
- Bring babies outside in strollers or baby carriages. Place babies on soft blankets, soft grass, or in play pens.

Move baby often from one area or activity to another.

- Make sure that baby doesn't get bored or fussy.
- Give babies a variety of toys and activities each day.
- Have enough things out for babies to play with at all times.
- Have low open shelves with safe toys for the crawling and walking babies to use on their own.

Repeat some old activities with new ones. Babies need the practice.

- Have baby do an activity two or three times in a week.
- Try the same activity with a different toy.
- Try the same activity in a different place.

Activity Tips

Talk to babies while they play. The more you talk, the more they learn.

- Tell them about what they are doing.
- Tell them about what they see, hear, feel, taste, and smell.
- Tell them what you and others are doing.
- Copy the sounds they make.
- Talk with expression. Try soft and loud, high and low, calm and excited voices.

Make everything you do count twice.

- Hold a tiny baby in your lap as you both watch the older babies. Talk to him about what they are doing.
- Use routine care as a special time to be alone with one child. Try doing some of the activities at this time.
- Remember to look into the baby's eyes as you talk. This gives each baby a turn to be special.
- Use the same materials to do more than one activity.
- Try the same activity with all the babies who are at the same level.
- Repeat a young baby's activity with older babies who are interested. The older babies still enjoy many of the ideas you use with the little ones.

Avoid safety problems.

- Cover electrical outlets, close the bathroom door, put safety locks on low cabinets, get rid of the toy box with a heavy lid that can crash down.
- Pick things up as you go along. Don't let things get too cluttered.
- Let the babies use toys that need to be closely watched only while you are there with them. Pick up older babies' crayons, play dough, and toys with many pieces when you have to go away.

Self-Directed and Teacher-Directed Activities

Remember to leave babies in their cribs only when they are asleep. When babies are awake, take them out of the crib and put them in an infant seat or on a blanket or soft clean rug in a safe play space.

Time for babies to play by themselves with safe toys outside of their cribs is important. This is true even for very tiny babies. Activities a baby can do by himself are called *self-directed* activities.

Some activities need you to be there with the baby, even after you get the baby started. We call these *teacher-directed* activities. Teacher-directed activities need to be planned for the times when you will be free to work with the babies.

Managing Teacher-Directed Activities With a Group of Babies

As you do a teacher-directed activity that you had planned for one baby, you will often be joined by a few other interested babies. The activity you may be doing with the one baby may not be right for the others. Keep baby from being interrupted by the others in the nicest way you can. Have toys nearby that the others can use. Have duplicates of the toy you are using so that the others can use them in their own way. Include the others in whatever you are doing with the one child whenever you can, and change the activity a bit to make it right for each child.

For example, if you are looking at a hard-page book with an older child and seeing if he will point to some pictures you name, have a few more sturdy books on hand for other babies who are interested. Include the baby who won't be put off by a book of his own. He may just want to look, listen, and be close to you. He will learn from seeing you and the other child talk about the book. Name some pictures and enjoy the book with both children but try extra hard to finish the activity you had planned.

Sample Schedule

Change this schedule to fit *your* babies' needs.

Children arrive:	Greeting Routine care (feeding, diapering, sleeping) Self-directed activities in play areas
Midmorning:	Planned play: teacher-directed activities for some, self-directed for others Nap for some, routine care for others Outdoor play
Late morning:	Lunch Nap for some Clean-up after lunch Teacher-directed activities for babies who are awake
Early afternoon:	Napping babies get up Routine care Planned play: teacher-directed activities
Mid-afternoon:	Routines Nap for some Teacher-directed activities for babies who are awake
Late afternoon:	Self-directed activities in play areas Routine care Talk to parents Clean up room Set up for next day

Making Spaces Safe and Healthy for Baby

If you do all you can to avoid health and safety problems, you will feel more relaxed and enjoy your work with infants more. Child proofing a room and an outdoor area takes a lot of thought. Think about what you can do to make it safe for babies all the time. Think about times when a baby is out of his crib playing with toys on his own while you are busy changing a diaper or washing your hands.

- Do not use toys that have small pieces with babies. There is too much danger of choking. Be super careful about this with toys babies use alone.
- Buy toys you can wash. Babies put everything into their mouths.
- Before using anything with a baby, check to see that no parts can come loose and be pulled off.
- Make sure all the materials and colors used in toys and furnishings are safe to suck on (non-toxic paints, fabrics, and dyes).
- Cover all electrical outlets.
- Make sure gates and doors are closed so that babies cannot go outside of safe areas.
- Check indoor and outdoor toys for sharp edges, splinters, and other dangers that develop as toys get older.
- Wash toys babies have used at the end of *every day* in soap and water. Use a strong liquid soap you can get in the drug store called *tincture of green soap*. Rinse well. Let toys dry in the air.
- Do not store toys in a toy chest with a heavy lid that can fall down. Use open, low shelves or activity boxes.
- Be sure to read the *Notes* in the activities for more health and safety ideas.

Writing Your Own Activities

Many of the activities in this book may be familiar to you. That's because some of them have always been used by parents and infant caregivers to help babies grow and learn. There will also be some activities you have never used before because no one can think of every activity or even remember all the ones they have done in the past. That's why activity books like this one help keep you on your toes with lots of new ideas. There may be some activities that you have enjoyed doing with infants that are not in this book. As you remember them, write them down in the blank activity boxes you will find at the end of each section. Then you will remember and use them as you write your activity plans.

When you work with babies, you will often find that you have to make up your own activities to meet their needs and make the best use of the toys you have on hand. Here are some ideas to help you write your own activities.

- First, think about what one child can do. Use the Baby Can lists to help focus on a skill that a child would like to practice or is ready to learn.
- Next, think about what you need to do to help the child practice the skill. Ask yourself the following questions.

  Will the activity be teacher or child-directed?

  What toys, materials, or other equipment will I need, if any?

  Where will the activity work well?

  How long will it take?

  How many children can take part?

  Will I have to get things ready ahead of time?

  Exactly what might I do to make the activity happen?

  What kinds of things can I say to help with baby's learning?
- Write your activity in an empty box. Try it out to see how it works. Make changes if you need to.

Making the Most of Your Space

There never seems to be enough usable space for play when you care for infants. All the things you need for routine care take up a lot of room. Planning how to use space can help, even though it may not do away with all the problems. Look around your room and ask yourself the following questions.

What can I store outside the room?

How can I move the furniture around to open up space for play?

How can I place things so that I can see all the babies at a glance?

Tips for Care

Use all the space you have. Put away anything you aren't using, such as extra cribs and highchairs.

Make sure routine care areas take up as little space as possible. Group highchairs so that they take up less space.

Place cribs so that they take up the least amount of floor space. (Remember that cribs should be about 24 inches apart to cut down on spread of germs).

Put the diapering table where you can see everything in the room while you change a baby. Try not to stand with your back to babies who are playing.

Tips for Play

Set up two safe, "fenced-in" open areas where babies can play on a blanket or rug. Having two areas keeps the babies out of each other's way.

Make sure the babies who can crawl or walk on their own have a large, open area for daily use.

Have plenty of easy-to-use toys in the play areas. Keep them on low, open shelves so that baby can get them on his own. Have two or more of the same toys. This will cut down on fighting.

Change the toys in the play areas often.

Set up only low things to fence in the play areas. This way you can see the whole room at a glance and get around quickly, but the babies will not be able to get out.

Stretching Space With Activity Boxes

When you put everything you need for one kind of activity into a box or dishpan you have made an *activity box*. This helps you keep many different things ready for children to play with without taking up much room. You can keep activity boxes in a closet or on a shelf, with a label on the box so that you know what's inside. Activity boxes help you get set up quickly because you won't have to run around at the last minute to find the toys you need.

Before you put things back into the boxes, remember to clean what you used that day. If you are careful to do that, you can count on anything you take out of an activity box being clean. Ideas for different activity boxes are listed below.

Activity Box Ideas

A *rattle box* has many safe, different rattles. This activity box is very good for making a center for babies up to five months old.

A *reaching box* has mobiles, cradle gyms, things firmly attached on strong yarn, and play things to bat at and reach for. It is a good idea to use reaching toys in only one of the play areas and to work out safe ways to hang the toys. You must keep babies who can pull up to stand out of this center while the toys are hanging unless you are there to watch them closely.

Touch, see, hear, or smell boxes have many textures, shapes, sizes, colors, sounds, or weights. Many of the activities in the sections "Activities for Learning from the World Around Them" and "Creative Activities" have games to play with the senses.

A *small muscle toy box* has busy boxes, things to pick up, and anything else for baby to use with his hands and fingers. Toys such as these make a very interesting center for the sitting and crawling infants.

A *musical activity box* has melody bells, drums, a xylophone, and other musical toys mentioned in the "Creative Activities" section. As you work with the music activities, you might want to make a few small music activity boxes for the different types of musical toys.

Doll, housekeeping, and dramatic play boxes have those toys needed for the dramatic play activities in the "Creative Activities" section. These toys can best be used with the sitting and crawling infants.

Making Interest Centers

An interest center is a place where babies have toys and space for a special kind of play. A soft toy center, a rattle center, or a music center are some examples.

The same interest centers do not need to be set up all the time. In fact, it is better to set up centers for a short time by bringing out different activity boxes. If you set aside two or more open play spaces, you can separate the more active babies who can crawl or walk from the babies who can't move around much.

You will want to have one play space where lying down and sitting infants can play on a soft blanket or a washable rug on the floor. This is not a safe surface for the infant who is trying to stand up and walk. He needs a flat floor for a firm footing. The younger infants also move around very little, so you might want to set up a good way to have low hanging toys for them to play with.

You will need to have a separate area for infants who can crawl or pull up and move around while holding onto furniture. Be sure to have sturdy furniture in this area to avoid falls and bumps. Also, have low open shelves with safe toys for these older infants to get on their own.

Be sure to set up an outdoor play space, too. Check to see that the area is safe and free of any health problems. Have weeds cut, be sure none of the plants are poisonous, and get rid of harmful bugs. Also, check the area daily, before you take the babies out, to see that it is safe and clean.

A fence around the area makes it easier to keep crawling or walking infants inside. It will also keep dangers out. A rolling cart or large carriage for taking out toys, blankets, or pads makes going outdoors easier. If you are doing a special activity or using large equipment, be sure to set up ahead of time. Once the outdoor area is set up, you will only need to get the infants out and back inside again.

Talking With Babies

To learn to talk well, babies need to be with caring adults who talk to them often and answer the sounds they make. Your job is to do both of these things to help infants in your care learn to understand and use words.

What do you say to infants?

From the time they are born, infants begin learning to talk by listening to the voices of the people who care for them. At only two weeks old, most babies will stop crying when they hear a favorite voice. Baby shows excitement by moving his arms and legs when you talk sweetly to him. You know he is really listening and enjoying what you say.

Babies need to hear words that tell about what they touch, see, hear, taste, or smell as they take in information through their senses. Then they will soon learn to put the words together with the right things and understand what people say. So talk to babies often about what they experience through their senses.

Babies also need to hear words that tell about their feelings — about whether they are happy, sad, excited, worried, or frightened. Whatever the feeling, you should try to give babies the words they will use later to tell about how they and others feel.

How do you answer baby's sounds?

The first kind of talking babies do is crying to tell you they need something — to be fed, or cuddled, or held up to see interesting things. You can answer their cries quickly to show that you care about what they have to tell you. A caregiver can learn to tell the different cries a baby makes and figure out what the baby is trying to say. Then she can say words for what the baby wanted as she answers.

At about two months of age a baby will talk by cooing as well as crying. Soon the baby coos with delight when he sees a favorite person. Caregivers should copy the baby's cooing, and later babbling, because many babies will make even more sounds when answered with the same sounds they are making.

How much talk is needed?

Children who talk well were talked to and listened to a lot as babies. To help babies grow into good talkers their caregivers and parents need to do lots of talking with them from the very beginning. In this book almost all activities have talking in them. There is a whole section called "Listening and Talking." The Conversations part of that section gives you ideas for things to talk about with babies all day long. It will not be enough to talk to a baby just one, two, or even ten times a day. Some talking you do with baby needs to be a part of activities you plan. Much more needs to be part of the many adult–baby conversations you will have all day long.

Finding the Right Activities

The activities for the first year of life have been broken into three age groups. Each one is shown by a baby picture.

 stands for what a baby up to five months old can do

 stands for what a baby from five to nine months old can do

 stands for what a baby from nine to 12 months old can do

Each activity has one of these three baby pictures near it. This makes it easy to pick out the right activities for each baby in your care. You can use these activities for a baby who is developing normally, more slowly, or faster than usual for his age. Just choose an activity based on what each baby *can do*. Each activity in this book tells what the baby should be able to do in order to take part in the activity.

The activities here are for babies who can do what is usual for up to 12 months of age. If your group has babies with abilities of children older than 12 months, you also need to use *Active Learning for Ones*.

On pages 26 to 28 you will find the Baby Can lists. These are lists of many things baby can do in each of the three age groups. Take time to look at these pages. It may surprise you to see how early babies develop many of their abilities.

Activity Guide

Look at the diagram below. It gives you an idea of how the activities in this book are written. By making use of underlining, italics, and pictures as short cuts, the activities tell you a lot in a few words. Each activity has a number and name.

There are also activity tips and notes that you should be sure to read in the activity sections. Some of the notes have safety tips and important practical ideas.

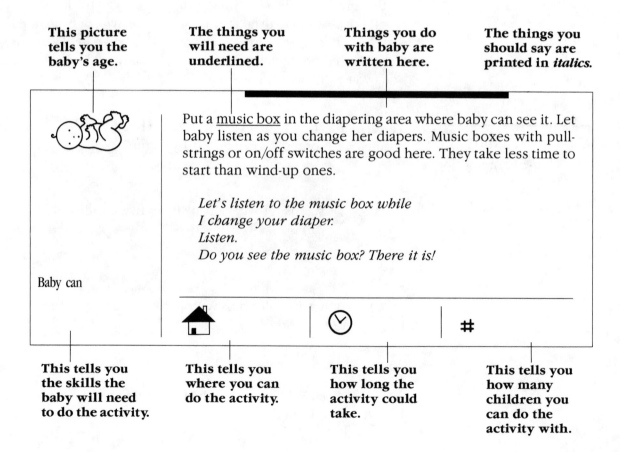

This picture tells you the baby's age.

The things you will need are underlined.

Things you do with baby are written here.

The things you should say are printed in *italics*.

Put a <u>music box</u> in the diapering area where baby can see it. Let baby listen as you change her diapers. Music boxes with pull-strings or on/off switches are good here. They take less time to start than wind-up ones.

> *Let's listen to the music box while I change your diaper.*
> *Listen.*
> *Do you see the music box? There it is!*

Baby can

This tells you the skills the baby will need to do the activity.

This tells you where you can do the activity.

This tells you how long the activity could take.

This tells you how many children you can do the activity with.

Planning for Infants

Writing An Activity Plan

It is easy to write a plan using the activities in this book. Each activity has a number and a name. Just put the number and name of the activity you want to use with each baby in the right place on the plan. You might be able to use the same activity for all those babies who are able to do the same things. Remember to put down the names of all the babies with whom you will be using the same activity. The written plan helps you to make sure that you are keeping each baby in mind. If anyone else has to take over for you, things will go more smoothly with a written plan.

Your written plan should list the *new* activities you want to try. But you might also want to repeat an old familiar activity that went well last week. Remember, babies enjoy doing activities over again.

The reason for planning is to be ready with a lot of activities and materials. This way the infants will be happy and will learn new things throughout the day, during routine care and at play times.

When you have written your activity plan, look it over and ask yourself:

Have I used routine care, such as diapering and feeding, to do activities whenever possible?

Have I planned for both morning and afternoon play?

Have I planned for outdoor play activities daily, weather permitting?

On the next two pages you will find samples of the Activity Plan form. If you are already using a written plan that you are happy with, by all means stay with it. Also, feel free to change this sample plan so that it fits your needs.

Activity Plan

Center or Home _____ Week of _____

Age Group _____ Caregiver _____

Fill in activity name and number and children's names in each box.

	Listening and Talking	Physical Development	Creative Activities	Learning from the World
M Monday	Sally 2 Pictures in the Diapering Area Leo 16 Playing with Picture Cards	Joey 56 Bicycle Push	Ray and Tonya 137 Colored Water	Emma 247 Crawling in the Grass
T Tuesday	Emma 13 Books for Baby	Sally 51 Where's the Rattle? Tonya 106 Sticky Tape Ball	Joey 126 Textured Cloths	Ray 299 What's Outside? 270 Toys Count
W Wednesday	Joey 20 Special Talking Time		Ray 161 Rock the Baby Leo and Emma 167 Play with Dolls	Sally 253 Look at Face Pictures Tonya 303 Tasting Treats
T Thursday	Ray 36 Questions and Answers Leo and Emma 42 Pictures on Wall or Floor	Sally 85 Grasp a Toy	Tonya 210 Where is Baby?	Joey 235 Hold Toy Animals
F Friday	Joey 6 Poems for Baby Tonya 11 Picture Peek-a-Boo	Ray 99 Pounding Toys Emma 79 Cushion Climb	Sally 177 Rock and Sing	Leo 339 Roll the Balls

This form has been filled in to show you how you can copy and use the form on the next page.

Planning for Infants

Activity Plan

Center or Home _____ Week of _____

Age Group _____ Caregiver _____

Fill in activity name and number and children's names in each box.

	Listening and Talking	Physical Development	Creative Activities	Learning from the World
M *Monday*				
T *Tuesday*				
W *Wednesday*				
T *Thursday*				
F *Friday*				

Planning for Infants

23

When You Start to Use the Activities

Before you start

Pick out the best Baby Can picture for each of your babies. This will help you plan for each baby and for a group of babies on the same level.

Look at all four activity sections and ask yourself the following questions.

Which activities do I have the materials for?

Which activities do I think each baby will be able to enjoy?

Which activities do I have time to do?

Which activities would I like to start with?

First week

- Plan one activity for each baby.
- Try to use each of the four activity sections.
- Use the activities you choose with as many babies as possible.
- Go back over the plan at the end of the week and ask yourself these questions about how things went.

Which activities went best?

Do I need to make any changes in the play spaces?

Do I need to make any changes in the daily schedule?

Do I need to make any new activity boxes?

Second week

- Plan one new activity for each baby.
- Repeat the old activities.
- Try each new activity more than once during the week so that you and the babies learn to do them well.
- Go back over the plan at the end of the week and ask yourself the questions about how things went.

Third week

- Plan at least two new activities for every baby.
- Fill in the activities you plan for each baby every day.
- Go back over the plan at the end of the week and ask yourself the questions about how things went.

Fourth week

- Plan some activities from each section for each baby every day.
- Fill in the written plan.
- Go back over the plan at the end of the week and ask yourself the questions about how things went.

Baby Can Lists

The next three pages give you more information on what infants can do. It is important to remember that these lists are only general guidelines to baby development and cannot be used to find out if a child is or is not developing normally. This is not a screening test. If you are worried about a child in your care, you should advise the parents to find a professional who can do some special tests. The parents could talk to their family doctor for some suggestions. Another way to find out about special services is through the child care professionals who come to your center.

The Baby Can lists help you become more aware of some of the things infants can do. The lists are actually made up of many of the Baby Can indicators in the activities. Without a list to follow it is hard to be aware of all the new little things a child learns to do. But it is these new little things that we need to encourage to help children grow and learn. These small advances are what we want a baby to practice as he plays with toys, looks at pictures, listens to our words, and takes part in all other activities. Then the big things will come more easily, in their own time.

Baby Can List

From newborn to five months, some things baby can do are

NEWBORN

- feel, taste, smell, and hear
- move arms and legs in play
- cry when in need of something
- enjoy being held and spoken to
- see things 8″ – 12″ away
- begin to turn head
- make eye contact
- look at clear simple pictures or designs
- grasp a small thing briefly
- make cooing sounds
- lift head to look around
- smile
- follow with eyes from side to side
- reach toward a toy
- show happy and sad feelings by making sounds
- sit supported, head steady
- turn head toward your voice or other sounds
- watch your mouth when you talk
- hold and shake a small toy
- see things farther than 12 inches away
- look at hands and feet
- bat or hit at things
- support head and chest with arms when on stomach
- try to roll over
- reach out when on stomach
- watch moving things
- answer a sound you make with another sound
- try to pull up to a sitting position
- bounce when held in a standing position
- enjoy looking in a mirror
- hold something in either hand
- play peek-a-boo

FIVE MONTHS
- recognize familiar people

Baby Can List

From five to nine months, some new things baby can do are

FIVE MONTHS
- look for things dropped
- uncover hidden things
- drop things on purpose
- hold a bottle*
- play with paper
- play with things by banging them together
- sit in a highchair
- change something from one hand to the other
- eat some solid foods
- reach out with one hand to pick something up
- sit without support
- support some weight when held in a standing position
- babble a string of sounds
- get into a sitting position
- begin to copy a few familiar sounds
- rock on hands and knees
- copy some familiar actions
- make noise with things on purpose
- pick up small things and put into mouth
- feed self finger foods
- babble to show wants
- copy some new sounds you make
- take things out of containers
- look at pictures when named
- pick up, push, or shove large things

NINE MONTHS
- pull a string

_____

* Make sure to hold and cuddle baby even when he can hold his own bottle. He needs your warmth and love. And remember—don't put baby to bed with a bottle. This can lead to ear infections, choking, or tooth decay.

Baby Can List

From nine to 12 months, some new things baby can do are

NINE MONTHS
- understand familiar words
- pull up to stand but not get down
- explore what is in a container
- drop things into a small opening or container
- wave bye-bye
- crawl, scoot, creep, or move well from one place to another
- crawl around and over things
- crawl while holding something
- follow a few simple directions
- poke at holes with pointing finger
- look at pictures in a book
- begin to stoop
- try to roll a ball
- babble as if speaking a sentence or asking a question
- tear paper
- say a few words, but not perfectly
- copy new gestures
- turn a few pages in a hard-page book
- begin to scribble
- roll or push a ball
- spend longer doing one thing than she used to
- make a stack of two blocks
- show interest in things farther away than he used to
- help pull off simple clothing
- fit one thing into another

12 MONTHS
- know where familiar things are kept

Activity Checklists

At the beginning of each activity section in this book, you will find a checklist. The checklist is to help you see how well the setting you create for children meets their needs for learning in that area. It's a good idea to try out these checklists to see what the strengths and weaknesses of your child care setting are for each type of activity in the book. Then you can see where improvements are needed and use the checklists as a guide for making changes.

You can do all the checklists at one time if you wish or pick one or two to work on at first and then do the others when you are ready. As you carefully read each statement on the checklists, look around your child care setting and think about the things you do with the children.

Carefully follow these directions as you do the checklists.

1. On each checklist you will find that the statements are followed by blanks under three age ranges. Note the ages of the children in your setting and rate the statements for those ages.
2. If you find much evidence that a statement is *true* for an age group, put a check in the blank.
3. If you find clear evidence that a statement is *not true,* put an X in the blank.
4. Make notes next to a statement if you are not sure about whether it should get a check or an X.

If people other than you want to use the checklists they will need to spend enough time observing in the room to really find out what they need to know. It takes about two hours in a morning to get most of the information needed to complete all the checklists. If the other observers do not see or hear everything needed to complete the checklists, then they will have to set aside time to ask you some questions about the child care setting. However, they should be sure to observe first.

Observers may see things differently from the way you see things. If there is a chance to talk about the differences, both you and the observer will probably end up with some good new ideas.

When You Want to Know More

Here is a list of some good materials to use when you wish to add to the ideas in this book. These are just a few of the many resources that are available to people who work with infants. Ask at your public library for help in finding the books that are listed, as well as other titles.

Caplan, F., ed. *The First Twelve Months of Life.*
This book discusses growth and development for each month and has a growth chart for motor, language, mental, and social development. New York: Bantam, 1978.

Castle, K. *The Infant and Toddler Handbook: Invitations for Optimum Early Development.*

A practical, hands-on guide for adults who care for children from birth through 24 months. Activities are easy to read, age appropriate, and include both the caregiver's role and the child's ability. Atlanta: Humanics Limited, 1983.

Cataldo, C. *Infant and Toddler Programs: A Guide to Very Early Childhood Education.*

This book discusses the history of infant and toddler programs, different types of programs for children of this age, how and what infants and toddlers learn, setting up and staffing infant and toddler programs, and ideas for activities. Reading, Mass.: Addison-Wesley, 1983.

Chase, R.A., et al., eds. *Your Baby: The First Wondrous Year.*

This book is divided into four parts: Parenting, Social and Emotional Development, Physical Development, and Play and Learning. The Play and Learning section includes "Designing your baby's environment" and suggests games for different ages. New York: Macmillan, 1984.

Karnes, M.B. *Small Wonder! 1: Activities for Baby's First 18 Months.*

This kit includes 150 activity cards grouped by age for each activity. Each card explains the purpose of the activity, lists materials needed, and gives step-by-step directions. Also included are 64 picture cards (with suggestions for stories and ways to use them), a caterpillar puppet, and a user's guide. The guide explains the materials; tells how to teach and play with a baby; and gives information on health and safety, child development, and using the kit with disabled children. Circle Pines, Minn.: American Guidance Service, 1979.

Moyer, I.D. *Responding to Infants.*

This book offers practical, easy-to-use activities for children from six to 30 months of age. Activities are divided into six areas: Fine Motor, Gross Motor, Intellectual, Social/Emotional, Language, and Self-care. Minneapolis: T.S. Dennison and Company, 1983.

Sparling, J., and I. Lewis. *Learning Games for the First Three Years: A Guide to Parent-Child Play.*

A series of 100 games that help children learn, grow and have fun with adults. The book is divided into six sections: 0-6 months, 6-12 months, 12-18 months, 18-24 months, 24-30 months, and 30-36 months. Each section begins with a checklist of developmental tasks. Each of the games has a brief description on the right hand page accompanied by a photograph, and a longer explanation on the left hand page. New York: Berkley Publishing, 1984.

Materials Index

The Materials Index lists the activities in this book by the toys, equipment, or other supplies needed for each activity. The index can be used in several ways. You can look for different activities to do with the toys you have. Or you can use the index as a guide as you make up a shopping list for your program.

F

Feathers: 232, 244
Fingerpaint: 144
Flashlight: 52
Flowers: 249
Food: 32, 102, 112, 174, 303, 319
Food coloring: 137, 139

H

Hats: 158, 160, 242
Hula hoop: 82

J

Jack-in-the-box: 217

K

Keys: 170

M

Mirror: 31, 60, 143, 160, 218, 278, 289
Mobiles: 82, 94, 121, 147, 233, 279, 327

P

Page holder, clear plastic: 142
Paper: 120, 129, 135, 138, 139, 141, 144, 294, 335
Pegs, 1/2–3/4″, board: 103, 108, 140
Piano, toy: 114, 212
Pictures: 1, 2, 3, 13, 16, 17, 18, 42, 122, 128, 133, 142, 262, 277
Pictures, of animals: 11, 121
Pictures, of cars: 17
Pictures, of flowers: 12
Pictures, of food: 14
Pictures, of people: 4, 9, 124, 163, 253, 306
Pictures, of shapes: 325
Pillows: 63, 82, 148, 171, 181, 188, 189, 191, 235, 266
Play dough: 140
Pocketbooks: 158, 170
Pots, pans, spoons: 99, 162, 196, 209, 259, 260
Puppet: 45, 168

R

Rattle: 25, 51, 54, 64, 89, 281
Records, tapes: 180, 202, 206, 222, 310
Ribbons, yarn: 50, 80, 92, 95, 121, 125, 131, 134, 142
Rocks: 252
Rug squares: 316

S

Seashells: 232
Scarf: 88, 96
Socks: 58, 91, 132, 301, 329
Spices, flavorings: 283, 297, 313
Sponge: 109, 139
Spray bottle: 139
Stacking rings: 343
String: 78, 95, 105, 184, 331

T

Tape: 144
Tea set, nonbreakable: 158
Telephones, plastic: 164
Toys: 36, 61, 63, 68, 70, 74, 75, 77, 78, 84, 93, 223, 257, 270, 328, 331
Toys, music or noise-making: 81, 90, 175, 178, 180, 184, 187, 191, 192, 197, 200, 203, 207, 211, 220, 226, 228, 293, 308
Toys, nesting: 116, 276, 341
Toys, pull-apart: 97
Toys, small: 85, 98, 104, 112, 115, 119, 208
Toys, soft: 79, 83, 90
Toys, teething: 259, 287, 320, 321
Toys, with holes (telephone, busy box, peg board): 110
Toys, with keys to press: 114, 212
Tray: 144

W

Walker: 61, 98
Water: 86, 109, 137
Wind chimes: 185

X

Xylophones: 201

Activities for Listening and Talking

Index
of Activities for Listening and Talking

Here's Why

*I*n order to learn to talk, a baby has to have other people talk to him. Babies learn to talk by listening, copying, and slowly making their own sounds into words that can be understood. At the same time that a baby is learning to talk out loud, he is also learning to think with words. This silent use of words is just as important as talking out loud because it will help him think and remember throughout his life.

This section pays special attention to the ways we can help babies talk and think with words. Babies learn more from adult talk when the adult looks into the baby's eyes while talking. There are activities in this section called conversations. In some, you talk to the baby so that the baby can listen and copy. In others, you listen to and repeat the baby's sounds. Other activities in this section use lots of pictures and books. These activities form baby's early experiences for later fun with books and reading.

Talking with babies is an important part of everything you do in daily care and play. In a way, each one of the activities in all four activity sections is a listening and talking activity. In each activity you are urged to talk about what the baby sees, does, and feels. The ideas in this section are meant to get you started as you help babies learn to talk and think with words. Activities in the other sections will give you more ideas for talking to babies as they play.

Materials and Notes
Books and Pictures

design pictures

hard-page picture books

dishpan of pictures

low book shelf

- When putting up pictures and mobiles remember that one- to two-month old babies see things best when they are between eight and 12 inches away. By two or three months, babies can see things that are closer or farther away.

- When hanging mobiles, watch to see where baby tends to look. Then put the mobile in that place.

- Even tiny babies get bored with looking at the same thing. Change pictures and mobiles often.

- Don't expect pictures to last forever. Keep lots of pictures on hand so that you can replace those that become torn or dirty.

- See if parents can help you collect pictures baby would like. Big clear magazine pictures, family photos, and pictures from children's books can all be used.

- Tell parents about the things baby is especially interested in. Show parents how their baby can look at pictures while you talk about what baby sees. Give parents some pictures for baby to look at and hear about at home.

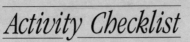

Activity Checklist
Books and Pictures

Book and picture activities for infants include use of colorful pictures and designs placed where children can see and touch, sturdy picture books, and simple picture games. Newborn babies see things best that are placed eight to 12 inches from their eyes. By three months of age, babies can see things that are closer or farther away. Infants enjoy pictures of faces and colorful designs that have lots of contrast between the dark and light colors. They look at colorful hard-page books and will be able to look at the pictures you name by the time they are one year old.

Check for Each Age Group	*0–5 mo*	*5–9 mo*	*9–12 mo*
1. Many pictures, some mobiles, and hard-page books are placed where children can easily see and touch.	—	—	—
2. Pictures are displayed safely (no thumbtacks within children's reach, etc.)	—	—	—
3. Pictures and picture books are colorful and show familiar things.	—	—	—
4. Pictures of people are not sexist and show different races and ages in a positive way.	—	—	—
5. Books children use are sturdy and have pages that are easy for children to turn (hard-page books).	—	—	—
6. Pictures, books, and mobiles are changed often.	—	—	—
7. Adult often points to, names, and talks with children about pictures.	—	—	—
8. Adult talks about picture books or reads every day with children, singly or in very small groups.	—	—	—
9. Adult plays simple age-appropriate picture games with children (covers picture for infant to uncover).	—	—	—
10. Adult asks simple questions about pictures to help children use or show understanding of words. (Adult: Where's the boy? Baby points to picture of boy.)	—	—	—

1

Baby can

- look at clear, simple, colorful pictures

Picture Place

Make a colorful collection of <u>large clear pictures</u> that will interest baby. Find different patterns of circles, bulls eyes, checks, faces, animals, and people. <u>Paste</u> the pictures onto <u>cardboard</u> and cover with clear <u>contact paper</u>.

Set up a picture place for baby. <u>Tape</u> some of the pictures on the wall and floor. Hang one above baby's head so that she can look at the picture, not at its edge. Put baby in the picture place. Pat one of the pictures and tell her about what she sees.

 indoors | 2–10 min | # 1–2 babies

2

Baby can

- look at pictures

Pictures in the Diapering Area

Hang <u>a few interesting pictures</u> in the diapering area. Put them on the wall where baby can turn his head to see. Or if there is a shelf overhead, tape one on the bottom side so that baby can look up at it as you change him. Cover the pictures with <u>contact paper</u> so that baby can touch and pat them freely. Point to and name the things baby sees.

That's a butterfly, Eric.
It has pretty pink wings.

 indoors | 1–3 min | # 1 baby at a time

3

Baby can

- look at pictures

Texture Pictures

Put up some <u>pictures that show different textures</u>. You can easily make a few by drawing or cutting out big clear pictures of animals, flowers, or faces, and then adding textures to them. For example, draw a simple bunny and paste a fluffy cotton ball tail onto it. Or make a big happy face and glue buttons on for eyes.

Put these where baby can see but not reach them. Make sure no baby can reach to pull off small pieces because they might cause choking. Talk about what baby sees.

 indoors | 1–3 min | # 1–2 babies

4

Picture Face Mobile

Draw a large colorful face onto each of <u>three cardboard circles</u>. Make all the faces happy but different in some way. Hang the faces from a <u>hanger or dowel</u> to make a mobile. Place baby on his tummy on a soft rug or blanket. Hang the mobile down low so that baby can see. Spin the faces gently so that they appear and disappear for baby. Try this in a gentle breeze, too.

What do you see, Tim? That's a face.
There's another face.

Baby can

- hold up head when on tummy

 in or out | 1–5 min | # 1–3 babies

5

First Pictures in a Book

Cuddle baby on your lap or close to you. Hold a <u>book with simple</u>, <u>clear</u>, <u>colorful pictures</u> so that both of you can see. Turn the pages for baby. Talk softly about what you see as you point to the pictures.

That's a picture of children playing.
See the boys and the girl.
That's a baby. Just like you.

Baby can

- look at pictures
- listen to your voice

 in or out | 1-10 min | # 1-3 babies

6

Poems for Baby

Choose a <u>book that has poems or rhymes</u>. The poems or rhymes do not have to be just for children, as long as you read so they sound soft and nice. Read quietly to baby. Try to put a little music in your voice to keep baby's attention. Cuddle baby or gently pat or stroke him as you read. Enjoy this quiet, relaxing time together.

Baby can

- listen to your words

 in or out | 1–10 min | # 1–3 babies

7

Watching Others With Books

When looking at <u>books</u> with older children, include baby in this activity. Put or hold him where he can see the pictures. Make sure he hears what you say while he sees other children enjoying books.

Here's the farmer. He's feeding the cow.
See the cow? Look, C.J., can you see the cow?

Baby can

- See things more than 12 inches away

 in or out 3–10 min # 1–3 babies

8

Seeing You Read

When you read things as part of your work throughout the day, call the baby's attention to what you're doing. Show her the thing you are reading. Tell her what you are doing.

How do I make this cereal for you, Latoya?
Hmmm. Let me read the directions.
See the directions on the box?
I'm reading them.
They tell me how to make your cereal.

Baby can

- watch what you do
- listen to what you say

 in or out 1–2 min # 1–6 babies

9

Pictures of People Baby Knows

Collect <u>pictures of people baby knows</u>. Cover them with <u>clear contact paper</u> to protect them. Hang them where baby can see and reach them. Try putting some low on walls and bookcases, on the back of the rocker where you sit with baby, or tied to legs of chairs or cribs. Place baby close to a picture where she can see it well. Talk about what she sees.

Look, Abby, Here's your mommy.
Who's she holding? That's you!

Baby can

- look at pictures
- know a few people

 indoors 1–2 min # 1–3 babies

10

Show a Picture — Sing a Nursery Rhyme

Look at a <u>hard-page nursery rhyme book</u> with baby. Make sure baby can see the pictures in the book. As you come to a rhyme you know, sing it for baby. If baby likes your song, sing it again. Don't worry about getting through the whole book. One or two pages may be enough.

Baby can

- listen to your voice
- look at pictures

 in or out | 5–10 min | # 1–3 babies

11

Picture Peek-A-Boo

Show baby a <u>big</u>, <u>bright</u>, <u>clear picture of an animal</u>. Try an animal he knows, such as a dog, cat, or bird. As he looks at the picture, cover it with a cloth. Ask where the dog went, then quickly take the cloth away.

Where's the dog, James? Where did it go?
There's the dog!

See if baby tries to move the cloth away when you do this. Share the delight baby feels each time he sees the picture.

Baby can

- look at pictures
- play peek-a-boo

 in or out | 2–5 min | # 1–3 babies

12

Picture Flower — Real Flower

Paste some <u>pictures of flowers</u> onto sturdy pieces of <u>cardboard</u>. Cover with <u>clear contact paper</u>. Show baby the flower pictures.

Look, Deedee. Flower. This is a flower.

Later, when you take baby out for a walk, point out real flowers for her. Or bring some flowers into the room and put them where she can see them.

We looked at flower pictures this morning.

Baby can

- look at pictures

 indoors | 1–3 min | # 1–4 babies

13

Baby can

- look at pictures
- play with a toy

Books for Baby

Cut out <u>large</u>, <u>bright</u>, <u>simple pictures</u> of things that will interest baby. Or draw and color some yourself. <u>Paste</u> the pictures onto sturdy cardboard. Cover with <u>clear contact paper</u>. Punch three holes in the side of each page. Tie three or four pages together to make a book. Place several books in a <u>dishpan</u> and put it on a low shelf for baby to reach. As she looks, help her turn the pages. Talk about the pictures.

See the flower? It's a big red flower.

 in or out | 2–5 min | # 1 baby at a time

14

Baby can

- eat solid foods
- look at pictures

Food Pictures

Draw or find <u>clear pictures of foods</u> baby likes to eat. Hang them near his eating place where he can easily see them. When feeding him a food, point out its picture. Try to make sure that the picture looks like the real food baby is eating. Pictures of finger foods, such as banana slices or crackers, are good. Talk about the picture and the food.

You're eating a banana, Andre.
See the picture of the banana?

 indoors | 1–2 min | # 1–6 babies

15

Baby can

- turn pages in a hard-page book
- look at pictures

First Book Area

Set up a book area for baby on a <u>low shelf</u> where she can reach. Put out eight or ten <u>hard-page books</u> for her to choose. Include books you make and books you buy. When baby chooses to play with a book, help her turn the pages and talk about what she sees. Make sure the books are put back where baby will be able to find them again.

You chose a book about puppies, Mei Li.
Doesn't this one look fuzzy and cute?

 indoors | 3–5 min | # 1–6 babies

16

Playing with Picture Cards

<u>Paste</u> small bright <u>pictures</u> onto sturdy <u>cardboard</u> cards. Cover with <u>clear contact paper</u>. Put the cards into a <u>plastic freezer container</u>. Give the container to baby to play with. Let her pour out the pictures and look at, hold, bend, or move them as she wishes. Tell her the names of pictures she looks at.

You have a picture of a train.
Toot! Toot! Toot! goes the train whistle.

Baby can
- empty a container
- pick up small things

 in or out | 2–10 min | # 1–2 babies

17

Labels in the Bottom of Dishpans

Put a <u>picture of a car</u> in the bottom of a <u>dishpan</u>. Cover it with <u>clear contact paper</u> so that baby can see it but cannot remove it. Place some <u>safe toy cars</u> on top of the picture. Give each baby a dishpan filled with cars to play with. As baby pulls out the cars, point to the picture of the car. (Try this with other toys, too.)

Look Andy. Here's a picture of a car.
These are little toy cars.
Sometimes you ride in a big car.

Baby can
- pick up things
- look at pictures

 in or out | 2–10 min | # 1–3 babies

18

Crawl on Pictures

Tape <u>big pictures</u> face down onto one to two yards of <u>clear, smooth vinyl floor covering</u>. Turn the plastic over, so that the pictures are face up and protected by the plastic. Let baby crawl on the plastic and look at the pictures. Talk about what she sees. Watch her carefully. Plastic can be slippery, especially for beginning walkers. Change the pictures every few weeks.

Oh, look at that shoe. It's a red shoe just like the one on your foot.

Baby can
- look at pictures
- crawl

 in or out | 5–10 min | # 1–6 babies

Materials and Notes
Conversation

rattles

squeeze toys

unbreakable mirror

baby doll

dishpan of pictures

puppets

- Even the tiniest babies listen when you talk to them. They listen and slowly figure out what all that talking is about. So talk to *all* babies as much as you can. Then babies will learn to talk more easily when the time comes.

- Babies try to talk to you in their own ways. So listen to the sounds they make and talk back to them. Answer them by repeating their own sounds or by talking about what you think they are trying to say.

- Babies get the most out of your talking when you talk about the things they see, feel, taste, smell, or hear.

- Most young babies listen best when you use a sing-song voice.

- Show parents how their baby gets excited when you talk to him. Help parents see baby's smiles, arms or legs moving, head turning, or eyes paying attention. Show them how easy it is to help baby learn to talk.

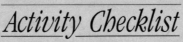

Activity Checklist
Conversation

Conversation activities for infants make use of the informal talking times adults have with children. Even the tiniest babies listen when they are talked to, and they talk back in their own ways. They watch the adult's mouth, move their arms and legs, or coo and gurgle in reply. For infants, crying is used as early talk. Children cry less as they learn that they can use words instead. By the time most children are a year old, they can understand familiar words and say one or two words.

Check for Each Age Group	*0-5 mo*	*5-9 mo*	*9-12 mo*
1. There is much talking to every child about what the child sees, feels, tastes, hears, or smells.	—	—	—
2. Adult makes eye contact when talking with child.	—	—	—
3. Adult talks to children about the routines and play they experience.	—	—	—
4. Adult has informal conversations with each child daily.	—	—	—
5. Adult responds to sounds infants make by imitating those sounds and describing what the baby is doing.	—	—	—

19

Routine Time Talks

While feeding, diapering, dressing, washing, or moving baby, talk to him. Tell him just what you are doing. Tell him what is happening to him.

Are you wet, Ron? Let me check your diaper.
You are wet. Let's go to the changing table.

Baby can

- hear the sound of your voice

 in or out | 1–5 min | # 1–6 babies

20

Special Talking Time

When baby is awake, cuddle her to help her feel safe. Then hold her so that she can watch your face. Talk to her for a little while. Look at her face as you talk. Say baby's name many times.

Mishu. Mishu. I see you.
You're such a tiny girl.
I see your eyes. You're really looking at me.
Mishu, you're such a nice baby.

Baby can

- listen to your voice
- watch your eyes and mouth when you talk

 in or out | 2–5 min | # 1 baby at a time

21

What Do Others Do?

Put baby in an infant seat where he can watch others work or play. As you do your work, stop often to talk to baby. Try to see what baby is watching. Name the things he sees.

What are you watching? Do you see Demetrius?
Demetrius is on the floor. He's playing with the doll.
Here's a doll for you, too.

Baby can

- follow moving things with eyes

 in or out | 1–2 min | # 1 baby at a time

22

Words for Baby's Cry

As you comfort baby when she cries, talk about why she is crying. Try to figure out what is wrong and tell her about it as you take care of her needs.

What's the matter, Karen? I know you're not wet, hungry, or sleepy.
Are you bored with that mobile?
Let's find something else for you to do.

Baby can

- cry when in need of something

 in or out | 1–2 min | # 1 baby at a time

23

Cooing Game

Listen for baby's cooing sounds. As he coos, answer him with the same sounds he is making. See if baby coos more and more when you join him in his sound game.

AH, OOH, OH, AH!
That's what you're saying isn't it, Carlos?

Baby can

- make cooing sounds

 in or out | 1–3 min | # 1 baby at a time

24

Baby's Happy Sounds

Place baby on her tummy on a soft rug or blanket. Sit near baby and slowly creep your fingers toward her. Then quickly and gently tickle baby. See if baby laughs or squeals.

Here come my fingers, Keia!
Here they come!
Closer, closer. They got you!

To change the game, make your fingers creep slowly or quickly, or wait different amounts of time before tickling baby.

Baby can

- show delight by laughing or squealing

 in or out | 1–3 min | # 1–4 babies

25

Listening and Answering

Shake a <u>bell</u> or <u>rattle</u> for baby to see and hear. See if he will coo or squeal when you do this. If he does, shake the toy again. Wait for him to coo. Shake the toy for every coo the baby makes. Try this same game with other sound-making toys. Don't worry if baby doesn't always coo for you. Shake the toy again and let him play with it in his own way.

Baby can

- make a sound after hearing a sound

 in or out | 1–5 min | # 1–3 babies

26

Words for Baby's Feelings

When baby shows her feelings by making different sounds, talk to her about what you think she's trying to say.

Yes! You like that dog, don't you.
You are so excited!

Baby can

- show feelings by making different sounds

 in or out | 1–2 min | # 1 baby at a time

27

Baby Greetings

When you greet baby, show her how happy you are to see her. Always talk with baby for a little while as you get her settled.

Good morning, Andrea.
Did you have a nice ride in the car?
What would you like to do now?
Do you want to sit here?
You can play with these cars.
And Thomas is here, too.

Baby can

- listen to you talk

 in or out | 1–2 min | # 1–2 babies

28

Watching Talking

Hold baby on your lap so that he can see your face when you talk. As you talk, let him feel your mouth moving. Let him feel the vibrations of your throat, the puffs of air, and the ways your mouth changes shape. Try making many sounds so that he can see, feel, and hear how they are different.

Puh, Puh, Puh.
Booo, Booo, Booo.
Eee, Eee, Eee.

Baby can

- watch your mouth when you speak
- reach for something

 in or out | 1–3 min | # 1–2 babies

29

Words for People Baby Knows and Sees

When someone baby recognizes is in the room, ask baby where that person is.

Where's Jonathan? Where's Jonathan?

When baby looks the right way, say something else about the person.

There he is! That's right.
Jonathan is feeding Tomika.

Baby can

- recognize familiar people

 in or out | 1–2 min | # 1–3 babies

30

Higher and Lower Sounds

When baby babbles, listen for changes in the high and low sounds he makes. Copy baby's sounds. Then let him babble again. See what baby does when the sounds you repeat are not quite the same as his. Try making the same high or low tone but not the same sound. For example, if baby says BA, BA, BA, BA, BA, BA, you say BEE, BEE, BEE, BEE, BEE. Laugh with baby and hug him for talking so nicely.

You really are trying to talk, Marcus!

Baby can

- babble high and low sounds

 in or out | 2–3 min | # 1 baby at a time

31

Talk to a Mirror

Look into a <u>mirror</u> with baby so that she can see herself and you. Talk to her reflection. See if she will watch your reflection as you talk.

I see you, Amanda.
There you are.
I see you in the mirror.

Make some funny faces in the mirror. See if baby will copy you in her own way.

Baby can

- enjoy his reflection in a mirror

 indoors | 1–3 min | **#** 1–3 babies

32

Foods Baby Eats

While feeding baby, tell him the names of the <u>foods</u> he is eating. Say the names simply a few times. Then say something else about the food.

Carrots. Carrots.
Mmmm. You like those carrots, don't you?
Now try some cereal. Cereal.
That's rice cereal.

Baby can

- eat some solid foods

 in or out | 1–5 min | **#** 1–3 babies

33

Sounds Baby Knows

Remember a sound baby likes to make like BA, BA, BA, or MA, MA, MA. When he is quiet, say the sound to baby. See if he will answer you with the same sound. Change the sound a little by making it quiet or loud, fast or slow, high or low. Watch baby's face to see what he thinks of these changes.

Baby can

- babble a string of sounds
- copy a sound you make

 in or out | 1–3 min | **#** 1 baby at a time

34

Baby can

■ babble to show
what he wants

What's Baby Trying to Say?

When baby babbles and gestures to tell you that she wants something, try to understand what she wants and answer her with real words.

What do you want, Rachel?
Oh. You want to get up.
Up you go.
You were tired of sitting there.

 in or out | 1–2 min | # 1 baby at a time

35

Baby can

■ watch as you move
around the room

Building Trust With Words

When you move away from baby to do other tasks, keep in touch with baby through your words. Tell baby what you are doing as he follows you with his eyes.

Jeremy, Jeremy. I'm just over here.
I'm cleaning the changing table.
I'll be done in a minute.
Now I'm washing my hands.
I'm going to feed Lucia now.

 in or out | 1–15 min | # 1–6 babies

36

Baby can

■ listen to your words
■ look at things you
pat or touch

Questions and Answers

As baby plays, help him learn the names of his <u>toys</u>. Ask him if he knows what the toy is as you touch it. When he looks at the toy, you can answer for him. He won't be able to answer yet, but he will start learning about questions, answers, and the names of things.

What's this, Brian?
It's a bear. Bear.
That bear is brown and fuzzy.

 in or out | 1–2 min | # 1–6 babies

37

Words for Same Things at Same Times

As you feed, change, dress, or put baby down for a nap every day, try to use special words for each activity, over and over.

Are you hungry? Do you want to eat?
You're wet. Let's change your diaper.
You ate it all. All done.
Do you want to get up? Up you go.

Watch to see if baby starts to understand these words.

Baby can

- listen to words you say

 in or out | 1 min | # 1–6 babies

38

Wave Bye Bye

When someone leaves, hold or place baby so that she can see them go. Have the person who is leaving say *Bye Bye* to baby. Say *Bye Bye* as you help baby wave.

After you have done this many times, see if baby can wave by herself or even attempt a bye-bye sound.

Look for the tiniest beginning of a wave. Baby may just move her fingers a bit.

You're trying to wave! Bye Bye, Cindy.

Baby can

- copy some gestures

 in or out | 1 min | # 1–3 babies

39

Does Baby Understand?

Before doing everyday things with baby, ask baby if she wants to. Say the words you have used over and over with baby as you have done these things.

Rosie, are you hungry? Do you want to eat?

Wait to see if baby shows she understands your words. She might look at the highchair or hold her arms out to be picked up. Say the words for baby that she cannot yet say.

Baby can

- listen and respond to familiar words

 in or out | 1 min | # 1 baby at a time

40

Ask and Show

Put a <u>few familiar things</u> in a <u>dishpan</u> for baby to see. Try a shoe, a doll, a ball, and a big wooden spoon. Ask baby where one of the things is, then pick it up to show him.

Where's the spoon? Where's the spoon?
Here it is! Spoon.
Where's the doll? Here it is! Doll.

Let baby play with the things in the dishpan. Name them for him as he plays.

Baby can

- pick up a toy

 in or out | 🕐 3–10 min | # 1–3 babies

41

More Ask and Show

Put <u>two things</u> into a <u>dishpan</u>. Choose things you think baby knows the names of. Ask baby where one of the things is. See if he will pick up the correct one.

Where's the spoon. Can you show me the spoon?
That's right. Spoon!

If he can't choose correctly, pick it up, smile, and name it.

Where's the spoon? That's the doll.
Here's the spoon.

Baby can

- understand a few words
- pick up a toy

 in or out | 3–5 min | # 1–3 babies

42

Pictures on Wall or Floor

Tape some <u>big bright pictures</u> covered with <u>clear contact paper</u> where baby can see and touch them. Place them low on the walls or even on the floor. Choose pictures of things that will interest baby, such as animals, other babies, clothes, or toys. When baby looks at the pictures, talk to him about what he sees.

What do you see, Nicky?
That's a cat. It has eyes and ears and a nose and a mouth.

Baby can

- look at pictures

 indoors | 1–3 min | # 1–6 babies

43

Names for Sounds

Help baby listen to and learn names for everyday sounds she hears, such as the telephone ringing, someone knocking at the door, or running water. When you hear a sound, talk about it with baby.

What is that? Do you hear that sound?
It's the telephone ringing. I'd better answer it.

Baby can

- listen to familiar sounds

 in or out | 1–2 min | # 1–6 babies

44

Dressing Words

Help baby learn the names of his <u>clothes</u> as you dress him. Give the word for each thing as you show it to baby and put it on him.

Let's put on your hat and mittens.
Here's your hat. It goes right here
on your head. And now one mitten.
Here it goes on your hand.
Where's the other mitten? Here it is.
Let's put it on your other hand.

Baby can

- understand familiar words

 indoors | 1–5 min | # 1–6 babies

45

Puppet Play

Put a simple little <u>puppet</u> on your hand and make it talk to baby. Have the puppet tell baby a little about itself. Let baby touch the puppet as it talks.

Hi, Leslie. My name is Brownie.
I am a dog. I am soft.
Oooh. I fell down. Waaaah. I hurt my nose.

Be as silly as you want to be with the puppet. Laugh and have fun with baby. Let baby play with the puppet if he wishes.

Baby can

- pay attention to a puppet

 in or out | 3–5 min | # 1–3 babies

46

Baby can

- listen to familiar words

Eyes, Nose and Mouth

Show baby the eyes, nose, and mouth on a <u>doll</u>. After showing one part on the doll, touch that same part on yourself and on baby. Take baby's hand and have her touch the eyes, nose, and mouth of the doll, you, and herself.

See the nose on the baby doll?
Here is my nose. And here is your nose.

 in or out | 1–5 min | # 1–2 babies

47

Baby can

- speak a few words

Baby's First Word

When baby tries to say a word, pick up on what baby is trying to say with excitement. Do your best to understand what baby means and answer him. For example, if baby says *Dada* when he sees his father, you might say:

Dada. That is your daddy!

 in or out | 1–2 min | # 1 baby at a time

48

Baby can

- speak a few words

More Words for Baby

When baby says a word, talk a little more with baby about what she is saying. Repeat what she said and add to her word.

Yes, Dorothy! Cup!
This is your cup!
You have milk in your cup.
Are you going to drink your milk?

Show delight in every new word baby learns.

 in or out | 1–2 min | # 1 baby at a time

Your Own Activities: Listening and Talking

Write your own activities on these three pages. You will find more information on writing your own activities in the Planning section, pages 12–13.

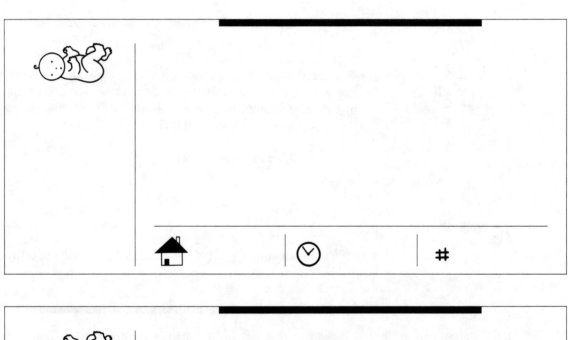

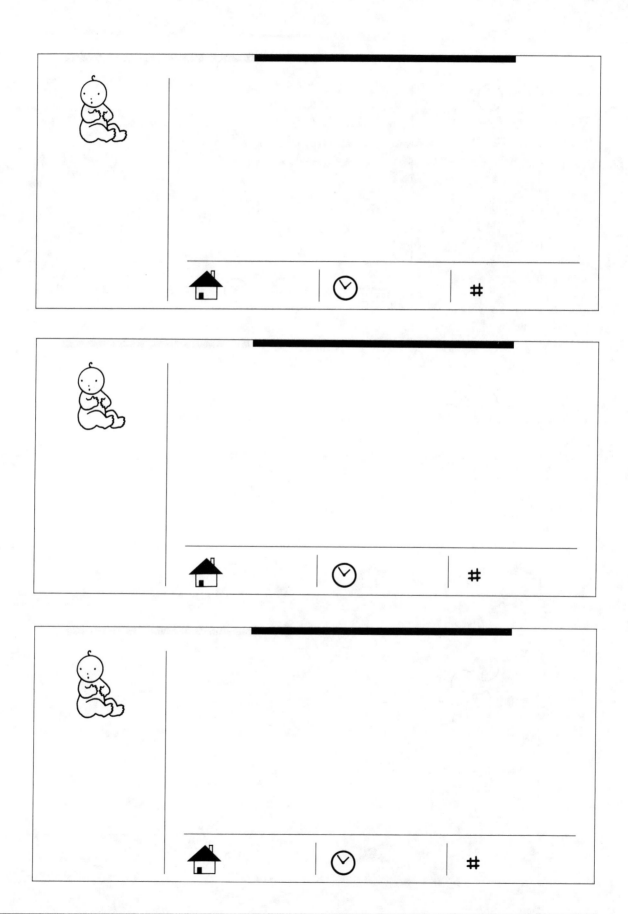

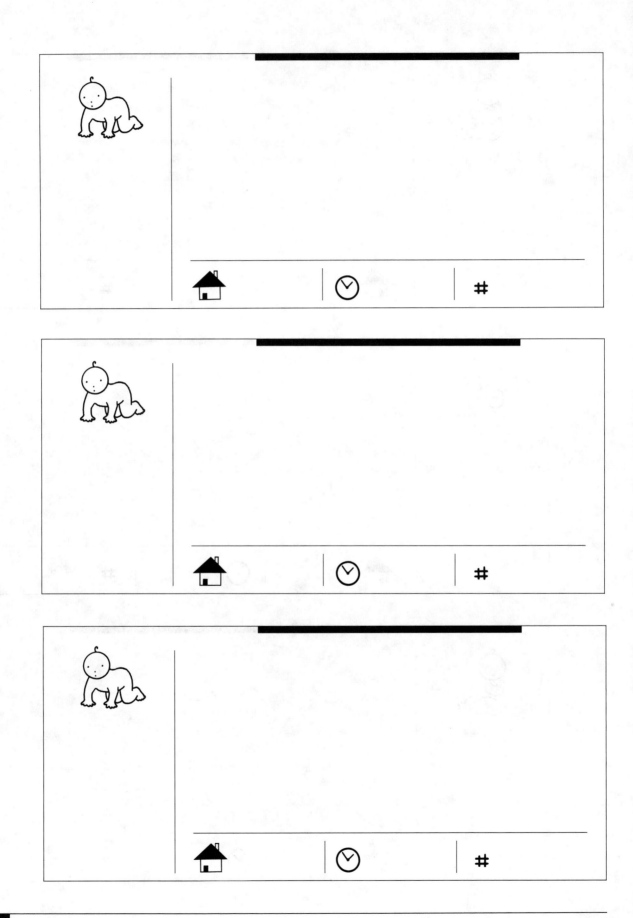

Activities for Listening and Talking

Activities for Physical
Development

Index

of Activities for Physical Development

Here's Why

*B*abies like to be active and to move whenever they get the chance. As their large muscles grow stronger, they learn to hold up their heads, roll over, reach, sit up, crawl, and walk. They also learn to use their small muscles to grab and to let things go, to pick up tiny things with their fingers, to hold things in both hands at the same time, and to get their hands to work together.

Muscles grow strong only when babies use them. The activities in this section make it more fun for babies to do things that use all of their muscles. In many of the activities you play with the baby so that both of you can enjoy the experience. These fun times help you and your babies become closer to each other.

Playing active games with babies also gives you a chance to use words to talk about what the infants are doing. Hearing you talk about something while he is doing it helps a baby learn to talk. Some physical activities give babies problems to solve, such as finding a hidden toy or reaching for something that is just out of reach. Solving these simple problems helps babies learn thinking skills. The happiness infants get from physical activities makes them feel good about themselves and about their growing abilities.

Materials and Notes
Large Muscles

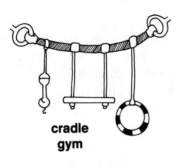

cradle gym

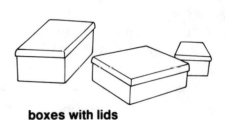

boxes with lids

rattles

soft dolls

roll for propping baby

- Babies learn to use their muscles by pushing up, reaching, crawling, or looking around at the things in their world. Having lots of interesting things for babies to see and hear will help them want to move and strengthen their muscles.

- When baby is very young and can't move around by himself, be sure to change his position often. Babies will get bored and tired of the same position or activity.

- Babies learn best when they have lots of freedom to explore. Set up your room so that there are many safe, interesting places for baby to move.

- Be sure to supervise the use of strings, balloons, beads, ribbon, or yarn. These things can easily hurt a child.

- Talk with parents about the many ways baby is learning to use her muscles. Share ideas with them about how to set up a safe floor space for the infant to play in and to move in the home.

Activity Checklist
Large Muscles

Large-muscle activities for infants include experiences in which the arm, leg, and body muscles are used and strengthened. For the youngest babies, turning and holding up the head, waving arms, and kicking legs are the first large-muscle activities. Later, large-muscle activities include crawling, climbing, walking, running, throwing, and balancing.

Check for Each Age Group	*0–5 mo*	*5–9 mo*	*9–12 mo*
1. Nonmobile babies are taken out of the crib and placed on safe firm cushioned surfaces where they can move freely (floor with carpet, blanket on grass outside, etc.).	—	—	
2. Nonmobile babies have positions changed often to encourage holding up and turning head, supporting chest on arms (place baby on stomach in a safe place near open toy shelf; later put in infant seat near busy boxes; etc.).	—	—	
3. Cradle gyms, busy boxes, and other toys to encourage reaching and kicking are accessible for baby's daily use.	—	—	—
4. Adult talks to children about the large-muscle activities children do.		—	—
5. Safe, open space is provided for the large-muscle play of crawlers and walkers, both indoors and out.		—	—
6. Safe, sturdy, age-appropriate large-muscle equipment is available for children's daily use, indoors and out (no-pedal riding toys, push-pull toys, balls, etc.).		—	—

49

Looking at Different Things Every Day

Place baby facing different directions on a <u>soft blanket</u>, <u>bean bag chair</u>, <u>or infant seat</u> on different days. Put baby in different places at different times. This will give baby new things to look at or a different way to look at the same things. Encourage him to turn his head or body toward the new sights and sounds.

Do you hear that birdie? He's singing you a song.
You can look out the window to see him.

Baby can

- begin to turn his head

 in or out | 10–15 min | # 1–6 babies

50

Swinging Colors

Tie a <u>pretty bead or stacking ring</u> to a <u>colorful ribbon</u>. Hang the ribbon over the changing table and swing it gently so that baby will move her eyes and head while you change her. Move the hanging ribbon to a different side of the changing area each week so that baby will turn her head or body to see it.

Look, Tamara. See the pretty yellow ring?
Can you watch it move?

Baby can

- begin to turn her head

 indoors | 2–7 min | # 1 baby at a time

51

Where's the Rattle?

Lay baby down on his back and shake a <u>rattle</u> gently near one side of his head. Encourage him to turn toward the sound. Shake the rattle again on his other side and encourage him to turn. Repeat the activity several times to give baby practice turning his head and using his neck muscles.

Do you hear that, Danny? It's a rattle!
Can you find that sound?

Baby can

- turn his head to find sounds

 in or out | 2–10 min | # 1–3 babies

52

Where's the Light?

Lay baby down on her back and shine a <u>flashlight</u> above her. Move the light slowly from side to side so that baby has to turn her head to watch it move. Make slow wide circles of movement with the light to give baby practice looking up and down, as well as side to side.

See the light. Can you watch it move?

Babies are usually interested in looking at lights, but if the light makes baby fuss, give her something else to look at.

Baby can

- follow moving things with eyes

 in or out | 2–3 min | # 1–4 babies

53

Shoulder Walk

Hold baby up with her head on your shoulder and walk around the room talking with her about the things she sees. Point to things above baby so that she has to lift her head to see them. Sit under a window, mobile, or picture. Help baby to lift her head and see the things of interest around her. Change shoulders so that baby has to turn and lift in different directions.

See the pretty picture, Toby?
Look up here. It's a picture of a puppy.

Baby can

- lift her head off your shoulder

 in or out | 2–10 min | # 1 baby at a time

54

Head Lifting

Place baby on his tummy on a <u>rug</u> or soft play area. Shake a <u>rattle</u> in front of baby for him to watch. Slowly lift the rattle just a little and encourage baby to lift his head and shoulders to watch it move. Raise and lower the rattle slowly as baby watches so that he can practice lifting his head and shoulders.

Find that rattle, Tommy. It's up high!
Look again and lift your head way up.

Baby can

- begin to push up on his arms

 in or out | 2–5 min | # 1–3 babies

55

Baby Balance

Support baby while he sits on your knees. Sway or rock gently and help baby practice balancing himself. With a younger baby, support the back and shoulders firmly. As baby gets older help him to support more of his own weight. Try moving your body other ways (rocking, swaying, bouncing gently) to help baby use different muscles and practice keeping his balance.

Bouncy, bouncy baby!
Up and down!

Baby can

- hold his head up

 in or out | 2–5 min | # 1 baby at a time

56

Bicycle Push

Lay baby on her back on a soft <u>rug</u> or play area. Put your hands under her feet and move her legs up and down, as if she were pedaling a bicycle. Smile and talk with her while doing this.

Up and down, up and down. You're riding a bicycle.

Encourage baby to push on your hands to strengthen her leg muscles.

Oh! You're so strong, Katerina! Push again.

Baby can

- push on your hands with her feet

 in or out | 2–5 min | # 1 baby at a time

57

Airplane

Play airplane with the baby held out in front of you. Swing him around slowly and fly him through the air like an airplane. Carry him over to see interesting things at different heights. Encourage him to lift his head or shoulders so that he can reach out to touch the things around him.

Whee! You're flying, Thien.
Get that flower!

Baby can

- lift his head
- reach out at toys

 in or out | 2–7 min | # 1 baby at a time

58

Kicking Bells

Securely sew <u>small shiny bells</u> onto the cuffs of <u>socks</u> or onto small circles of <u>elastic</u>. Slip a pair of cuffs around each baby's ankles and shake her feet to make the bells jingle. Encourage baby to do lots of kicking.

Kick, kick, kick. Do you hear those bells, Mary?
Make them ring again.

Baby can

- kick her feet

 in or out | 2 – 10 min | **#** 1 – 6 babies

59

Cradle Gym

Place a <u>cradle gym</u> or <u>sturdy mobile</u> about six inches above each baby. Help baby to hit at it with her hands, arms, and feet.

Kick the butterfly, Jan!
You got it! Kick it again.

Baby can

- kick her feet
- reach toward things

 in or out | 5 – 15 min | **#** 1 – 6 babies

60

Exercise with a Mirror

Hold baby so that he faces away from you. Carry him over to a <u>mirror</u> and talk with him about what he sees. Stand about a foot away from the mirror and encourage baby to lean forward and pat the mirror. Help him to pull himself back up so that he again leans on you. Lean back and forth several more times to help baby strengthen his back and stomach muscles.

Touch that baby! See the baby in the mirror!

Baby can

- reach out to grab things
- hold head steady

 indoors | 2 – 10 min | **#** 1 baby at a time

61

Baby in Walker

Place each baby in a <u>sturdy</u>, <u>well-balanced walker</u> so that he can sit up and even move around a little. Put out <u>safe toys</u> for him to reach, either on the walker tray or on low shelves or tables. Make sure the area has a clear flat floor space. Be sure other babies are out of the way. (As soon as baby begins to crawl, put the walker away so that baby will get lots of crawling practice.)

You reached the clown by yourself, David!
That was good walking.

Baby can

- sit supported

 in or out | 5–20 min | # 1–4 babies

62

Roll Over With Help

Place baby on her back on a <u>soft carpet or blanket</u>. Sit or kneel on one side of her. Gently pull her far-away leg over to you so that she starts to roll over onto her tummy. If she follows her leg with the rest of her body let her finish rolling over by herself.

Over you go! You rolled over, Sherry!

If baby doesn't show signs of turning her body, help her do this and roll her over. Take care to pull very gently and help baby as soon as you see she can't follow her leg.

Baby can

- begin to roll over

 in or out | 1–3 min | # 1 baby at a time

63

Reach for the Toy

Help baby sit on a <u>soft rug</u> with a <u>pillow</u> behind her so that she won't get hurt if she falls back. Place a few <u>toys</u> in front of her so that she has to bend and reach to pick them up. Let her play on her own with the toys while you talk to her about what she is doing.

You have the ball now, Rebekah.
Good girl! You picked it up all by yourself!

Baby can

- sit supported

 in or out | 3–5 min | # 1–3 babies

64

Rolling From Back to Front

Lay baby on his back and shake a <u>toy</u> or <u>rattle</u> over him. Encourage him to reach up and grab the toy. After he lets go, shake the toy again. But, as baby reaches for it, slowly move the rattle across his body, away from his hand, so that he must reach farther. Keep practicing this reaching activity until baby rolls himself over trying to get the toy. Let baby catch the toy often. Later put baby on his tummy and help him roll to his back.

Come on, you can do it. Reach for the rattle, Jacob.

Baby can

- begin to roll over

 in or out | 2–10 min | # 1 baby at a time

65

Bouncing

Stand baby up on your knees and bounce her gently up and down. Let her support as much of her own weight as she can to help strengthen her leg muscles.

Bouncy, bouncy baby!
Jump, jump, jump!

Baby can

- support some of her own weight

 in or out | 3–5 min | # 1 baby at a time

66

Rocking Game

Sit baby on your lap facing you. Lean her back slightly and help her to pull herself back up. Make up a game or song to go with this rocking motion. This activity will help baby strengthen her stomach muscles.

Rock, Michelle, rock! Pull back up to me.

Baby can

- begin to pull herself up to sit

 in or out | 2–7 min | # 1 baby at a time

67

So Big

Seat baby on a soft <u>rug</u> and sit down in front of her. Give her a finger from each hand to hold and say:

How big is Marsha? So big!

As you say *So big,* raise baby's arms up over her head. After you have played the game a few times, see if she will raise her arms on her own. Raise your arms over your head for her to copy.

Baby can

- move her arms up and down

 in or out | 2 – 10 min | # 1 – 6 babies

68

Leaning Over a Roll

Fold a <u>towel or blanket</u> in half and roll it into a thin log-shaped roll. Lay baby on his tummy over the roll and give him <u>a few toys</u> to look at and play with. Move the toys from side to side so that baby has to reach a few inches to get the toy he wants. Make sure baby can get the toy after he reaches a few times.

*You want that truck? Reach way over here, Raul.
You can do it. I know you can!*

Baby can

- push himself up on his forearms or hands

 in or out | 2 – 10 min | # 1 baby at a time

69

Swinging Animals

Help baby sit on a soft <u>rug</u> or play area. Hang a <u>small stuffed animal</u> from a <u>hook, rod, or crib rail</u> so that it swings about 12 inches off the ground. Gently swing the toy animal in front of baby and encourage her to reach out or catch the toy.

Get the monkey, Ellen. You can get it!

Try this activity with baby in different positions. Turn her sideways so that she can reach around to get the toy. Or lay her on her back so that she can kick the toy.

Baby can

- hit at moving things

 in or out | 2 – 10 min | # 1 – 3 babies

70

Turn and Find

Sit with baby in a soft play area or on a <u>blanket</u> outside. Show him <u>a favorite toy</u>. After you have his attention, lay the toy down, either beside or behind him. Encourage baby to turn his body around and find the toy.

Where's that telephone, Carl?
Can you find it?

Baby can

- turn to see things

 in or out   5 – 10 min   # 1 – 6 babies

71

Beach Ball Fun

Sit baby in a soft play area and roll a <u>big beach ball</u> toward her. Encourage her to put her arms out to get the ball and push it back to you. Use a ball that is at least 12 – 16 inches across so that baby has to make big wide movements with her arms.

Here it comes, Debby. Catch the ball.
Now push it back to me.

Baby can

- reach up to grab a large toy

 in or out   5 – 15 min   # 1 – 6 babies

72

Copy Cat

While baby is sitting in his highchair, play a little copycat game with him. Do simple actions in front of him and try to get him to copy you: Bang on his tray with your hand or spoon; clap your hands; pat your head or chest; tip your head from side to side; stamp your feet.

Clap your hands, Jimmy.
Make big claps with your whole arm.

Baby can

- copy a few movements

 in or out   2 – 5 min   # 1 – 6 babies

73

Crawling Stretch

Kneel on your hands and knees beside a crawling baby. Begin to rock back and forth or from side to side. Slowly stretch up and back in long catlike stretches to practice using different muscles. As you move your body, see if baby will try to move his in the same way beside you.

Stretch way out. There you go.
We look like stretching cats.

Baby can

- kneel on hands and knees

 in or out | 2–5 min | # 1 baby at a time

74

Scooting

Lay baby on his tummy on a soft <u>rug</u> or play area. Shake <u>a toy</u> in front of him just out of his reach and then put it down on the rug. Encourage him to scoot forward and get the toy.

Come on, Darin. Scoot up here and get the keys.
I know you can do it.

Baby can

- begin to scoot

 in or out | 5–15 min | # 1–4 babies

75

Toys in New Places

Spread <u>toys</u> around in different areas of the floor. Put baby down on the rug where there are no toys and then show her where the toys are. Encourage her to scoot or crawl over to the new toy places.

Look, Juanita. The cars are over there by the sink.
Can you crawl over and get them?

Baby can

- crawl to a toy

 indoors | 5–15 min | # 1–6 babies

76

Baby can
- crawl

Crawling Races

Get down on your hands and knees beside baby. Crawl a little ahead of him, then turn and call for him to follow.

Come on, Ricky. Come catch me.

Laugh and talk a lot with baby while you are racing. See if he will follow you all around the room. If you don't feel you can crawl, then bend down, face baby, call to get his attention, and move away as you get him to follow.

 in or out | 2–10 min | # 1–4 babies

77

Baby can
- crawl to a toy

Toy Toss

Sit on the floor with baby in your lap and toss <u>a favorite toy</u> out in front of you. Encourage baby to crawl after it and bring it back to you. When baby is tired of playing with that toy, toss another one a few feet away and again encourage him to crawl over to it.

Go get the train, Leon. I know you like that toy.

 in or out | 2–10 min | # 1–6 babies

78

Baby can
- crawl after moving things

Toys on a String

Tie an <u>interesting toy</u> to the end of a <u>string</u>. Gently pull the string in front of baby and encourage her to crawl after it. Be sure to let baby catch and play with the toy every minute or so. Otherwise she will get frustrated very quickly and lose interest.

Catch the clown, Emily.
Look, it's moving across the room.

Watch carefully, or remove the string from the toy so that baby can play safely.

 in or out | 2–10 min | # 1–3 babies

Activities for Physical Development

79

Cushion Climb

Lay a few old sofa cushions on the floor in a soft area for baby to climb on. Spread a couple of soft toys behind the cushions to attract his attention. See if he will climb over the cushions to get the toys.

Crawl up here, Peter.
Come get the block.

Note: Be sure to watch baby very closely; he might lose his balance and fall.

Baby can

■ crawl over things

 in or out | 5–15 min | # 1–6 babies

80

Ribbons Reach

Sit in a chair in front of baby. Tie long colorful ribbons around your knees and shake them in front of her. Encourage baby to pull up to a stand as she reaches up to play with the ribbons.

Do you see the yellow ribbon, Abby?
Can you stand up to get it?

Baby can

■ begin to pull to a standing position

 in or out | 2–10 min | # 1–3 babies

81

Dropping a Noisy Toy

While baby stands, holding onto your legs or a piece of furniture, drop a noise-making toy onto the floor beside him. Encourage him to stoop or to bend over and pick it up.

See the bell, Alan?
Can you bend over and pick it up?

Baby can

■ begin to stoop

 in or out | 2–10 min | # 1–4 babies

82

Obstacle Course

Set up a little obstacle course for baby to climb on and play in.
Try laying out a few of these things:
a <u>hula hoop</u> to crawl through
a <u>pillow</u> to crawl over
<u>beach balls</u> to push away or crawl around
<u>boxes</u> to crawl in and through
<u>cardboard blocks</u> to pile up
<u>mobiles</u> or hanging things to hit at

Baby can

■ crawl around and
over things

 in or out | 5–20 min | # 1–6 babies

83

Pulling Up for Toys

When baby begins to pull up to stand, move some <u>soft</u>, <u>light-weight toys</u> to a shelf at least 16–20 inches high. Show baby the new place for toys and encourage her to pull up and get the toys all by herself.

Stand up, Carrie.
You can get that doll all by yourself now.

Baby can

■ pull up to a
standing position

 indoors | 2–10 min | # 1–6 babies

84

Hide'N'Seek

Put a big <u>empty cardboard box</u> in front of baby. While she watches, drop <u>a favorite toy</u> into the box. Help baby find the toy and get it out of the box.

Where's that bell, Tammy?
Can you find it?

Watch baby enjoy pulling, shoving, and moving the box around to get the toy out.

Baby can

■ pull up to a
standing position

 in or out | 2–10 min | # 1–4 babies

Materials and Notes
Small Muscles

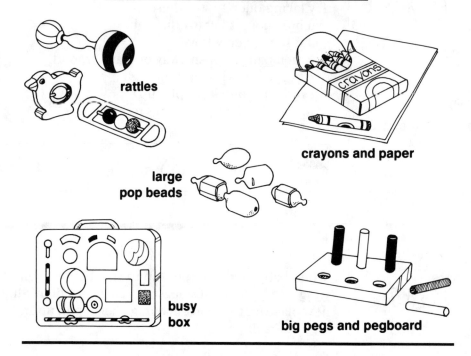

rattles

crayons and paper

large
pop beads

busy
box

big pegs and pegboard

- Babies learn the most about their world by touching, mouthing, and holding the things they see. Be sure to give baby lots of safe, interesting things to look at and to hold.

- Babies have fun holding and feeling things of many different textures. Let them play with things that feel hard, soft, fuzzy, smooth, squishy, or rough.

- Place many interesting things around the room so that baby can learn to reach and grasp. Babies need lots of practice as they begin to use their eyes and hands together.

- Watch baby very closely when you give him small things to hold. Be sure they are too big for him to swallow so that he won't choke.

- Give parents ideas about safe mobiles or cradle gyms to hang up at home for their child to use. These help baby begin to use his eyes and hands together.

Activity Checklist
Small Muscles

Small muscle activities for infants include experiences in which children learn to control hand and finger movements. At first babies have little control over the small muscles. They can hold a toy put in their hand for a little while, then drop it. Soon babies discover their hands and watch their movement with interest. They learn to pick up and drop things at will, change something from one hand to the other, and pick up tiny things. During this time, babies need lots of toys to hold, to shake, and to explore with their hands and fingers. Later, as eye-hand coordination improves, children will enjoy pull-apart and put-together toys.

Check for Each Age Group	*0–5 mo*	*5–9 mo*	*9–12 mo*
1. A variety of safe toys for children to hold, to shake, and to explore with fingers and hands are accessible for children to use by themselves daily.	—	—	—
2. Safe small-muscle toys are organized by type and stored on low, open shelves for children's free use.	—	—	—
3. Small-muscle toys are changed regularly.	—	—	—
4. Duplicates of popular toys are available.	—	—	—
5. Adult shows children how to use small-muscle toys as needed (shakes rattle for child to copy; shows child how to stack cubes; etc.).	—	—	—
6. Toys are clean, in good condition, and washed daily.	—	—	—
7. Protected space is set aside for play with fine-muscle toys (form board on a small rug, stacking cubes on a child-sized table, etc.).	—	—	—
8. Children are encouraged to feed themselves finger foods daily.		—	—

85

Grasp a Toy

Rub a <u>small toy or block</u> across the palm of baby's hand for him to grasp. As baby wraps his fingers around the block, let him hold onto it.

Here's a block, Robby. Can you hold it?

Baby can

- begin to grasp small things

 indoors or out | 2–5 min | **#** 1 or 2 babies

86

Water Drops

While baby is lying on a rug or sitting in his infant seat, drop <u>a few drops of water</u> onto the palms of his hands. Talk with baby about what you did. Help him to open and close his hand as the water drops.

Oh! That's cool water, isn't it, Kim?
Can you close your hand and hold onto that drop?

If baby shows that he does not like this activity, stop, cuddle him, and try another activity.

Baby can

- close his hand

 in or out | 2–10 min | **#** 1–3 babies

87

Finger Wiggle

Play "This Little Piggy" with baby's fingers. Wiggle her fingers as you say the rhyme and clap her hands together when you finish.

This little piggy went to market.
This little piggy stayed home.

Baby can

- look at fingers and hands

 in or out | 2–5 min | **#** 1–3 babies

88

Scarf Pull

Gently pull <u>a long scarf or string</u> across the palm of baby's hand. Encourage baby to close her hands around the scarf and hold onto it.

Do you have my scarf?
Hold on tightly or I'll pull it away.

Note: Put the scarf out of baby's reach when you are done with this game.

Baby can

■ begin to grasp things

 in or out │ 3–5 min │ **#** 1–2 babies

89

Moving Rattle

While baby is lying on her back, shake a <u>rattle</u> in front of her. After you have her attention, move the rattle slowly to one side. Make sure she is still watching and then slowly move it all the way back across her body to the other side.

Can you follow the rattle?
Watch it closely. Where did it go?

Baby can

■ watch something move from side to side

 in or out │ 2–5 min │ **#** 1 baby at a time

90

Squeeze Toys

Find some <u>small</u>, <u>very soft toys that make a noise when squeezed</u>. Hold one up in front of baby and squeeze the toy while he watches. Give the toy to baby to play with and to practice squeezing. Make sure that the noise-maker can not be pulled out and swallowed.

Squeeze the duck. You can do it.
Make that noise again.

Try squeezing other noisy things, such as wrapping paper.

Baby can

■ close hands around a toy

 in or out │ 2–10 min │ **#** 1–6 babies

91

Face Socks

Very securely sew <u>bright little pieces of material or buttons</u> in the shape of a face onto a <u>sock</u>. Slip the sock over baby's hand and move it a little to get her attention. Encourage her to watch the sock and touch the pieces of material.

What can you see? Is that a face looking at you?
Can you get that face?

Be sure baby does not put the buttons or small pieces of material into her mouth, especially if baby has teeth.

Baby can
- look at her hands

 in or out | 2–10 min | # 1 baby at a time

92

Ribbon Wristbands

Securely sew <u>several two to three inch brightly colored ribbons</u> to a small wristband made of <u>sturdy elastic</u>. Slip the elastic band around the baby's wrist and gently shake her hand to catch her attention. Encourage her to watch and pull at the ribbons.

Do you see that red ribbon, Thelma?
Can you reach up and touch it?

Be sure the wristband is not too loose or tight for baby.

Baby can
- look at his hands

 in or out | 2–10 min | # 1–2 babies

93

Holding Two Things at the Same Time

Put into a <u>dishpan</u> a few <u>small toys</u> that baby can hold in one hand. Give baby two toys, one at a time, to hold. If he drops a toy, hold another one up to his empty hand for him to grasp.

Here's a block, Benji.
Can you hold another one?
Now you have two.

Baby can
- hold small toys in either hand

 in or out | 5–7 min | # 1–6 babies

94

Grab the Mobile Toy

Place baby on her back under a <u>mobile that has toys that go around</u>. Use a separate mobile for each baby. Hang the mobile so that the toys are just within reach of baby's fingertips. Wind up the mobile so that the toys begin to circle over baby. See if baby reaches up and tries to grab the toys as they go by.

Get the bunny, Rebekah!
Now try to get the frog.
Here comes the bunny again!

Baby can

- grasp small things

 in or out   2–10 min   **#** 1–2 babies

95

Threaded Blanket

Loop and securely tie many <u>five-inch pieces of string or colored yarn</u> through the middle of an <u>old blanket or quilt</u>. Put baby on top of the blanket and show him a piece of string. Help him to find and pull on other pieces of string all by himself.

See the string, Vernon?
Reach for it and pull it hard.

Baby can

- grasp small things

 in or out   5–15 min   **#** 1–6 babies

96

Ribbon Pull

Hang a <u>long</u>, <u>brightly colored ribbon or scarf</u> loosely around your neck. When you lean over baby to change him or pick him up, allow him to reach out and to touch the ribbon or scarf. Try adding a securely tied <u>wooden bead</u> to each end of the ribbon. Smile and talk with him about what he's doing.

You got the ribbon, didn't you?

Baby can

- reach out for things

 in or out   2–7 min   **#** 1–2 babies

97

Pull-Apart Play

Gather a few different kinds of <u>pull-apart toys</u> and put each set into a <u>small bin or dishpan</u>. Use toys such as big popbeads, shape blocks that fit on a stick, or stacking rings. Put a few of the toys together for baby and give them to him to hold, play with, and pull apart.

Oh! You pulled those apart!
Do you want me to put them back together for you?

Baby can

- pull small things apart

 in or out | 2–10 min | 1–6 babies

98

Pick Up and Move

Put rows of <u>small</u>, <u>safe</u>, <u>colorful toys</u> where baby can reach when in a <u>walker</u>. Put some on low shelves, on a chair, or on a low table. Put the toys in different places around the room so that baby can discover them and them pick up as she moves around in the walker. Be sure that there is a clear path to the toys. Put toys that baby drops back up for her to discover again.

What did you find, Becky?
You picked up the rubber kitty!

Baby can

- move in a walker
- pick up small toys

 in or out | 3–10 min | 1–3 babies

99

Pounding Toys

Gather <u>toy mallets</u> or <u>plastic hammers</u> or <u>spoons</u> for baby to bang with. Give him noisy things to bang on, such as <u>pots</u>, <u>pans</u>, <u>or drums</u>. Help baby grasp a mallet and bang. Try using things to bang with that have handles of different sizes so that baby learns how to grasp and to hold things in different ways.

Bang! Bang! Bang! Bang the pot, Brett.
Yea! You did it!

Baby can

- grasp different sized handles
- bang things

 in or out | 3–7 min | # 1–6 babies

Activities for Physical Development

100

Baby can

- grab small things

Grabbing Out of a Can

Put some two-<u>inch cubes</u> in the bottom of <u>large plastic containers.</u> Give one can to each baby and help her reach in, grab the toys, and pull them out.

What do you have?
Did you find a block in that can?

 in or out 1–10 min # 1–2 babies

101

Baby can

- eat finger foods
- pick up little things

Find the Cereal

Put a <u>piece of cereal</u> in the bottom of a <u>cup</u> or <u>small plastic bowl</u>. Give baby the bowl and tell her to scoop out the cereal.

Get the Cheerio, Norma.
Reach in and scoop it out.
M-m-m! Doesn't that taste good!

Give baby several more pieces of cereal so that she can practice picking up small things.

 in or out 2–7 min # 1–6 babies

102

Baby can

- pick up and eat finger foods

Slippery Foods

When baby is sitting in his highchair, give him <u>small pieces of slippery foods</u> to pick up and eat. Try soft peaches, pears, bananas, fruit cocktail, or other foods that are harder for baby to pick up and hold. Be sure to help baby if he shows signs of getting upset.

Can you pick up the peach?
It's slippery, isn't it? Hold on tight.

 indoors 2–10 min # 1–6 babies

Activities for Physical Development

103

Baby can

- grasp things

Pegs and Pegboards

Give each baby a <u>pegboard</u> with <u>fat pegs</u> (1/2″–3/4″ wide) to pull out. If she doesn't pull them out on her own, show her how to do it and help her pull them out. Give her a <u>plastic bowl</u> to put her pegs in as she pulls them out of the pegboard.

Where's the peg, Emma? Can you find it?
Pull it out.

 in or out | 2–10 min | **#** 1–2 babies

104

Baby can

- change things from one hand to the other

Hand to Hand

Give baby <u>a small toy</u> to hold in one hand. After she has played with it for a minute or so, hold <u>another toy</u> up to that same hand. Try to get baby to move the first toy to her other hand instead of dropping it. Then give her the new toy to hold as well. Let her play with the two toys together.

Can you take this block, too?
Put that one in your other hand.

 in or out | 2–7 min | **#** 1–4 babies

105

Baby can

- pull on small things

One-Bead Necklace

Make a long necklace out of <u>sturdy string</u> and <u>one large bead</u>. Wear it around your neck while you play with baby or change his diaper. Let him play with the bead. Show him how to slide it back and forth on the string.

You have my necklace.
Can you pull the bead around?

 in or out | 1–3 min | **#** 1 baby at a time

106

Sticky Tape Ball

Make a small ball (2″–3″) out of <u>masking tape</u>, sticky side out. Stick it onto baby's hand or clothes. See if she will pull it off or move it from hand to hand.

That's a sticky ball, isn't it?
Can you pull it off your hand?

Watch to make sure baby does not put the ball in her mouth. The glue will not hurt her, but tiny pieces of tape may cause choking.

Baby can

- grasp small things

 in or out | 1–10 min | # 1–3 babies

107

Poke the Egg Carton

Securely glue <u>small pieces of colorful textured material</u> in the bottom of each section of an <u>egg carton</u>. Give an egg carton to each baby to poke and feel.

Can you put your finger in here?
That cloth feels soft and fuzzy.

Baby can

- poke with one finger

 in or out | 1–7 min | # 1–3 babies

108

Finding the Peg

Help baby sit on a <u>clean shag rug or fuzzy carpet square</u>. Drop a <u>peg</u> or <u>toy</u> into the rug while baby watches and encourage her to pick it up.

Can you find the peg? It's down in the carpet.
Pick it up.

Note: When using small toys with babies, be sure to watch them very closely so toys won't be swallowed.

Baby can

- pick up small things

 indoors | 2–10 min | # 1–3 babies

Activities for Physical Development

109

Water Play

Help baby sit in a <u>small pool or tub</u> with about half an inch of <u>warm water</u> in it. Give her <u>small cups</u> to fill and pour, <u>spoons</u> to stir the water, and <u>sponges</u> to squeeze. Talk with her about what she's doing.

Squeeze the sponge, Kathy.
Oh! Doesn't that water feel good.

Note: Never leave baby alone in the water.

Baby can

- squeeze a sponge

 in or out | 5 – 15 min | # 1 – 6 babies

110

Poking Holes

Give baby <u>toys with holes</u> in them to poke and to feel with his fingers. Use toy telephones, busy boxes, Chinese checker boards, peg boards or make some of your own by cutting holes in sturdy cardboard lids or boxes. Make sure the holes are large enough so that baby's finger won't get stuck. Be sure there are no sharp edges, too.

Poke the telephone dial, Charlie.
It has a round hole.

Baby can

- poke with one finger

 in or out | 2 – 10 min | # 1 – 6 babies

111

Turning Hard Pages

Look with baby at <u>picture books that have heavy,</u> <u>thick card-board pages</u>. As you look at each picture, talk about what you see and then let baby turn the page by himself. You may have to help him turn the pages one at a time.

What do you think comes after this picture?
Can you turn the page and see?

Baby can

- try to turn pages in a hard-page book

 in or out | 3 – 10 min | # 1 – 3 babies

112

Baby can

- find a toy hidden under a cloth

Finding a Hidden Toy

While baby is watching, hide a <u>favorite small toy</u> under a cloth. Encourage baby to grab the cloth, pull it away, and find the hidden toy.

Can you find the duck?
Pull the cloth away and let's see what's there!

Try this with safe <u>finger foods</u>, too.

 in or out | 2–10 min | # 1–2 babies

113

Baby can

- hold two small things at the same time

Banging Together

Give baby <u>two blocks</u>, one in each hand. Hold two blocks in your hands and bang them together as baby watches. Try to get baby to copy you and bang his blocks together. After he can bang two blocks, give him two things that are a little harder to hit together, such as two spoons or two smaller blocks.

Hit those blocks, Sammy.
Bang! Bang! Bang!

 in or out | 2–7 min | # 1–4 babies

114

Baby can

- poke with pointing fingers

Pressing Keys

Let each baby play with a pop-up toy, toy piano, or another <u>toy that has keys to press</u>. Show her how to use her fingers to press down the small keys. Help her to use her fingers rather than her whole hand.

Press right here, Serena.
Click, click, click.
Do you hear the sound it makes?

 in or out | 3–10 min | # 1–6 babies

Activities for Physical Development

115

Drop in the Boxes

Make simple drop-in boxes for baby out of <u>shoe boxes</u>. Cut a hole in the top or side of a box for baby to poke things through. Then give him <u>safe</u>, <u>small toys</u> to drop in his box. Try blocks, pegs, cars, balls, or other small toys.

Where did you put that car?
You put it in the box, didn't you?

Baby can

- drop things into a container

 in or out   3–15 min   # 1–3 babies

116

Nesting Cups

Give baby <u>two or three cups that all fit inside of each other</u>. Try measuring cups, margarine tubs of different sizes, nesting blocks, or plastic bowls. Show baby how the toys fit together. Then see if baby will copy what you did.

Put the cup in here, Dick.
See, they fit together.

Baby can

- put things inside each other

 in or out   2–10 min   # 1–2 babies

117

Stacking Blocks

Give baby two or three <u>blocks of different sizes</u> to stack and knock down. Hand him the blocks one at a time and help him to pile them on top of each other. Make a game out of playfully knocking them down and laughing as you build them up again.

Put it up here, Johnny.
We have two blocks on our pile.

Baby can

- stack things

 in or out   2–10 min   # 1–4 babies

118

Holding Three Things

Sit in front of baby with a few <u>small blocks or toys</u>. Hand them to baby one at a time and try to get him to hold three toys at the same time.

Here, Douglas. Can you hold another block?

Baby can

- hold at least two small things

 in or out | 2–5 min | # 1–6 babies

119

Dump the Basket

Play a dumping and filling game with baby. Put a few <u>little toys</u> in a <u>small basket or plastic bowl</u>. Show baby how to pick up the basket and turn it over so that the toys fall out. Laugh when they fall and tell baby what happened.

Oh, look! They all fell out!
Can you put them back in, Rosa?

Give the basket to baby and help her dump and fill by herself.

Baby can

- fill and empty a container

 in or out | 2–10 min | # 1–4 babies

120

Beginning to Scribble

Give baby <u>a fat crayon</u> and some <u>paper</u>. Draw a few lines while she is watching and then try to get her to scribble on her own.

Make a mark, Megan.
You can color on the paper.

Baby can

- begin to scribble

 in or out | 2–7 min | # 1–3 babies

Your Own Activities: Physical Development

Write your own activities on these three pages. You will find more information on writing your own activities in the Planning section, pages 12–13.

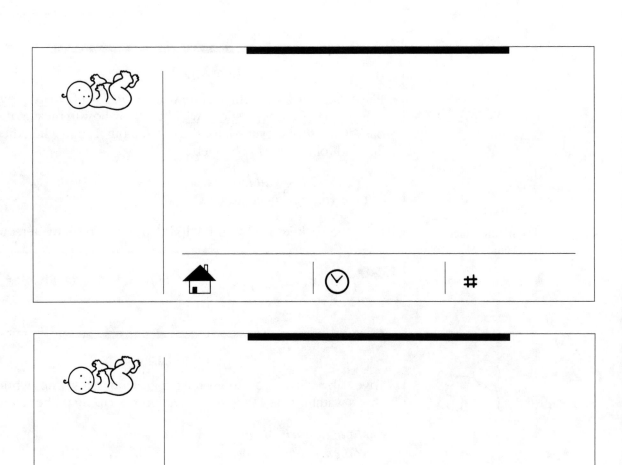

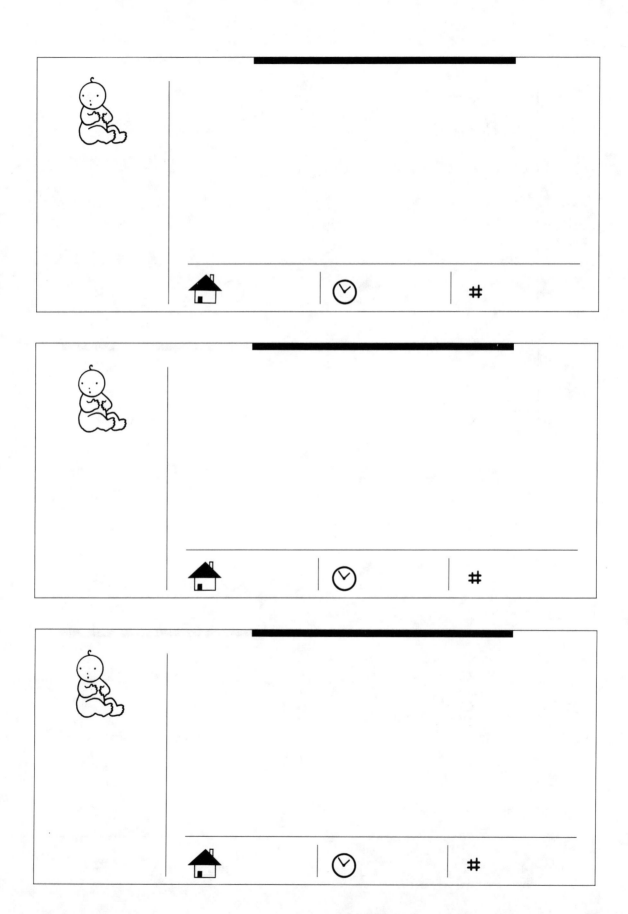

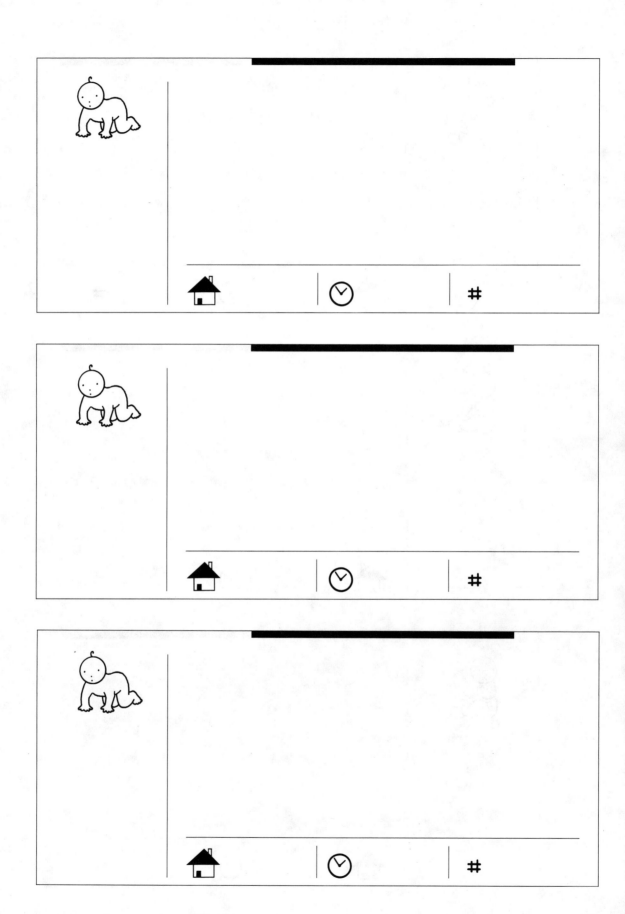

Creative Activities

Index
of Creative Activities

*T*he activities in this section give babies their first chance to enjoy music, art, block play, and dramatic play. Music is one of the first ways you and baby can listen to and talk to each other. Moving to music seems a natural way to show love to babies. To hold a baby and move back and forth with him is relaxing for you as well as for the child. Songs help babies fall asleep or surprise them into laughter.

Both art and block activities help babies learn what they can do by themselves. Art begins for babies as they watch brightly colored mobiles or raise their heads to see the pictures you put up. They learn more about art as they have chances to make things change around them. Making a brightly colored ribbon tied to their wrist flutter in the air, crumpling a piece of paper, or making a mark with a crayon are baby art activities. Ideas for block building begin as babies find out how blocks look, feel, stack, and fall.

Babies can start to take part in dramatic play as they use toy dishes, dolls, hats, and toy animals. You can make believe with babies about the things they see and do every day. The baby who is held every day can make believe by holding a baby doll. The baby who is afraid of a real dog can pet the fuzzy toy dog you hold. The baby who isn't allowed to go into his mother's purse can go through a play pocketbook. Make believe is a safe way for children to explore their feelings and ideas.

From these simple beginnings, creative activities develop into important aspects of children's play.

Materials and Notes

Art

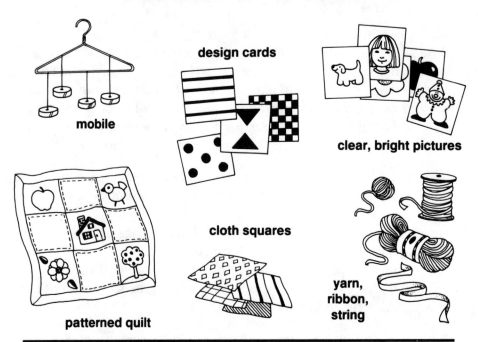

mobile

design cards

clear, bright pictures

patterned quilt

cloth squares

yarn, ribbon, string

- Be sure to change pictures often. Babies show much interest in new things.
- Include people pictures that show many cultures and ages, both male and female.
- New babies can see best when toys, mobiles, and pictures are about 12 inches from their eyes.
- New babies enjoy looking at faces, checkerboards, spirals, dots, stars, or other bold patterns.
- Keep a close watch on baby when using any string, yarn, or ribbon.
- Hang pictures and mobiles securely. Baby will try to put anything into his mouth.
- Share some baby art activities with parents. Encourage them to talk with baby at home about how things look and feel.

Activity Checklist
Art

Art for infants includes things put up for them to look at as well as materials given to them to feel. At the beginning, babies respond to brightly colored objects and pictures close to them. Later, the feel of different textures becomes important to babies. Interest in handling art materials usually starts between 12 and 18 months. This is when the child can start to use drawing materials, fingerpaints, and play dough.

Check for Each Age Group

	0–5 mo	5–9 mo	9–12 mo
1. Large, clear, brightly colored pictures of people and familiar things are placed where child can see them, especially at child's eye level.	—	—	—
2. Brightly colored things of different sizes and shapes are placed where child can see and touch them.	—	—	—
3. Pictures, mobiles, and other objects for looking and touching are changed often.	—	—	—
4. Adult talks to child about shape, color, and textures of things that the child experiences and sees.	—	—	—
5. Child is encouraged to feel, handle, and explore different textures (fabrics, papers, toys).	—	—	—

121

Mobiles

Make <u>simple mobiles</u> for baby to look at. Hang them over cribs, changing tables, or anywhere else in the room where baby can see. If you hang them over play areas, make sure they are low enough for baby to watch but out of older baby's reach. Hang things about 12–15 inches away from youngest babies. Try making mobiles using some of these ideas: pictures of animals; pictures of familiar things; brightly colored pieces of paper or ribbons.

Baby can

- look around

 indoors | 1–15 min | # 1–4 babies

122

Pictures Around the Room

Put up different <u>pictures</u> in your room for baby to look at. Change these pictures often so he doesn't get bored. Cut out pictures of familiar things, people, and animals from catalogs, books, or magazines. Try to get pictures showing lots of different colors, textures, scenes, and faces. Put up pictures that you like, not just those made for babies.

Look, Aaron. Do you see that pretty farm house?
The barn is red, and the trees are green.

Baby can

- look at pictures

 indoors | 1–5 min | # 1 baby at a time

123

Looking at the Light

When you see baby turn his head to look at a <u>light</u>, talk with him about what he sees.

What do you see? You're looking at the light, aren't you?
That's the light on the ceiling.

Make sure the lights are not too bright for baby to watch. Let him look at sunlight moving on the floor, lights with solid shades around them, or ceiling lights that are far away from his eyes. Make sure baby is free to turn away when he wishes.

Baby can

- look around

 indoors | 1–10 min | # 1 baby at a time

124

Faces

Cut out <u>big pictures of people's faces</u> from magazines. Cover them with <u>clear contact paper</u>. Securely attach them to chair legs, table legs, low wall space, or any other open space at baby's level for her to watch or pat. Put her on her tummy so that she can see the pictures. As she looks at a picture, talk with her about what she sees.

That's a face. See the lady's nose?

Baby can

- look around

 indoors   2–10 min   # 1–4 babies

125

Ribbons and Yarn

Cut 6″–8″ pieces of <u>brightly colored ribbon or yarn</u>. Tie these around chair legs, crib bars, table legs, or other areas baby can see. Get close to baby as he looks at these bright colors and gently blow the ribbons so that they move. Talk with baby about what he sees.

That's a red ribbon. See it move, Sabrina?
Isn't it pretty!

Baby can

- look around
- reach toward things

 in or out   1–5 min   # 1–2 babies

126

Textured Cloths

Find <u>cloths of different textures</u> (slippery satin, bumpy wash-cloths, soft cotton) and gently rub them over baby's arms or legs. Talk with her about what she feels. Name the feelings for her.

How does that feel? It is soft, isn't it?

Make sure you do this activity slowly and gently so that baby will not be frightened by these new feelings.

Baby can

- feel things around her

 in or out   1–5 min   # 1–3 babies

Creative Activities

127

Baby can

- raise head to look around

Patchwork Quilt

Place baby on her tummy on a <u>brightly colored patchwork blanket or quilt</u>. Show her some of the patterns and talk with her about them.

This is red, Lashawn.
It has little dots all over it.
See?

Help baby focus in on other patterns of the quilt. Talk as you show them to her.

 in or out | 2–15 min | # 1–5 babies

128

Baby can

- look at things close by

What Do You See?

Carry baby around the room and talk about all the different <u>pictures</u>, <u>colors</u>, <u>or designs</u> she can see. Hold baby in your lap while you do an art activity with an older child. Talk with baby about what she is watching.

See, Bessie. Todd is playing with play dough.
It's green and feels squishy.

 in or out | 1–5 min | # 1–2 babies

129

Baby can

- look at things close by

Peek With Color

Sit with baby facing you. In front of your face, hold up a <u>brightly colored piece of paper with a picture, a pattern or a design on it</u>. Play peek-a-boo with baby as you hide behind your paper and then move it away from your face. Move slowly enough for baby to have time to look at your picture color or design.

Peek-a-boo, Ruthie. Here I am.

 in or out | 2–10 min | # 1–4 babies

130

Textured Toys

Sew together a few <u>pieces of different textured material</u> for baby to play with or give baby a block or ball with different textures on each side. As baby plays with the cloth, help him touch all the different textures. Talk with him about what he feels.

That's the shiny side, Juan.
It feels smooth.

Baby can

- hold and drop things

 in or out | 2 – 10 min | # 1 – 3 babies

131

Colorful Wrist

Loosely tie a <u>brightly colored ribbon</u> onto baby's wrist or ankle where she can easily see it. Help baby move her arm or leg so that the ribbon attracts her attention. Talk with her about the color and how it moves.

Look at that ribbon, Carrie. See it move.

Make sure to remove the ribbon when baby tires of the activity. Try making little wrist bands of different textured materials too.

Baby can

- look at fingers, hands and feet

 in or out | 2 – 15 min | # 1 – 4 babies

132

Colorful Socks

Find old <u>adult socks</u> that are brightly colored or have interesting patterns on them. Pull one of them half way over baby's hand. Then move her hand in front of her face so it attracts her attention. Talk with baby about what she sees.

It's blue, Nancy. See it move?
Look at the pretty lines on your hand.

Try socks of different textures, too.

Baby can

- look at fingers and hands

 in or out | 2 – 10 min | # 1 – 5 babies

133

Baby can

- look at pictures

Your Own Picture Books

Make picture books for baby to look at. Cut out <u>pictures</u>, <u>paste</u> onto <u>cardboard</u>, and cover with clear <u>contact paper</u>. Tie or fasten three or four pictures together to make the child's own book. Talk with baby about the pictures.

Look at the kitty. She's brown and fuzzy.

Try making books about many different things such as colors, shapes, people, or animals.

 in or out | 2–10 min | # 1–4 babies

134

Baby can

- watch moving things

Patterns

Draw some <u>different-sized shapes</u>, such as circles, triangles, or squares. Use <u>wide, brightly colored pens</u> on <u>white paper.</u> Punch a hole into each design and tie a <u>brightly colored ribbon or string</u> through the hole. Hang these so baby can watch them move. Try hanging them over the changing table, from a swing, or from a tree branch outside.

 in or out | 2–15 min | # 1–6 babies

135

Baby can

- tear paper

Tearing Paper

Give baby <u>pieces of paper</u> to tear. Try using paper of many different colors and textures. Talk with baby about what she is doing, how it feels, and how it looks.

See? You're tearing the paper, Keiko.
Now you have two red pieces.

For a picture to hang up, have baby drop her torn pieces onto a sheet of paper with glue already on it. Hang baby's work where she can see it.

 in or out | 2–10 min | # 1–4 babies

136

Feeling Texture Books

Make a texture book by gluing <u>pieces of cloth</u> on both sides of 5-inch <u>cardboard</u> squares. Punch two holes along one edge of each square. Then tie the pages together with some <u>sturdy string or ribbon</u> to make a book. Make sure that the pages facing one another have different textures, such as soft and hard, rough and smooth, fuzzy and slick, spongy and flat.

This is bumpy like a washcloth.
Can you feel that, Penny?

Baby can

- use fingers to feel things

 in or out | 2–5 min | # 1–3 babies

137

Colored Water

Have baby sit in a <u>highchair.</u> Put a bib on her and roll up her sleeves. Pour <u>a little water</u> on the tray and drop a few drops of <u>food coloring</u> onto the water. Gently pat the water for baby. If she copies what you did, talk with baby about what she is doing.

Look, Latarsha. You're patting the drops.
See the blue move around.

As soon as baby loses interest, dry her off and take her out of her highchair.

Baby can

- copy a few actions

 in or out | 1–5 min | # 1–2 babies

138

Scribbling

Securely <u>tape</u> a <u>large piece of newsprint</u> onto the floor. Place baby on the paper and give him a <u>fat crayon</u>. Draw a few simple lines as he watches you. See if he will copy your actions. If he does not, gently hold his hand and help him scribble.

Look Ron, you made a picture. See the colors?

If baby tries to eat the crayon, gently tell him *"No, crayons are for drawing."* If he continues to put the crayon in his mouth, take it away and give him a toy he likes to play with.

Baby can

- begin to scribble

 indoors | 1–5 min | # 1–5 babies

139

Baby can

■ copy a few actions

Spraying Colors

Securely tape a <u>large piece of newsprint</u> onto a low wall space. Fill a <u>spray bottle</u> with <u>water</u> that is deeply colored with non-toxic <u>food coloring</u>. Spray the paper while baby watches. Give baby a two-inch piece of <u>sponge</u> and help her to pat the paper as the water drips.

Catch that drop. Pat, pat, pat.
See the pretty color.

 in or out | 2–5 min | # 1–4 babies

140

Baby can

■ use fingers to explore and poke

Play Dough

Help baby sit at a table or in her highchair. Press some <u>play dough</u> onto the table in a flat pancake shape. Poke your finger into it to make a few holes while baby watches. Help her poke or pat the play dough. Try giving her a <u>large peg or blunt stick</u> to poke holes into her dough.

See, Tina. You made a hole.

Note: Watch baby carefully to make sure she doesn't eat the play dough.

 indoors | 2–10 min | # 1–4 babies

141

Baby can

■ squeeze paper

Crumpling Paper

Give baby a <u>small piece of paper</u>. Hold another piece in your hand as baby watches.

Look at my paper. It's all crumpled!
Now squeeze your hand!

Help baby to crumple his paper and make a big game out of what you are doing. Try it another day with paper of a different size, color, or shape.

 in or out | 2–10 min | # 1–5 babies

142

Picture Holders

Place <u>pictures baby likes</u> into <u>clear plastic page holders</u> that can be found in stationery, office supply or photography stores. Punch holes in the edge of the plastic holder. Then tie the page securely with <u>yarn or ribbon</u> where baby can see and touch. Put baby's own scribble pictures in the page holder for her to look at, too. Talk about all the pictures as baby looks.

That's a picture of a woman, Denise.
And that's a crayon picture you made.

Baby can

- look at pictures
- scribble with a crayon

 indoors | 1–3 min | # 1–2 babies

143

Colored Reflections

Cover an <u>unbreakable mirror</u> with <u>smooth colored see-through cellophane gift wrap</u>. Play with baby in front of the mirror where he can easily see himself. Talk about the colors and the baby in the mirror. Try different colors on the mirror at different times or different colors next to each other on the same mirror.

See that baby, Pascal? That's you!
You look all blue in the mirror.

Baby can

- enjoy looking in a mirror

 indoors | 1–5 min | # 1–3 babies

144

Handprint Art

Put a thin layer of <u>nontoxic fingerpaint</u> onto a <u>tray or paper plate</u>. Put a <u>big bib</u> on baby and put her into a <u>highchair</u>. <u>Tape</u> a piece of <u>paper</u> onto the highchair tray. Ask baby to pat her hands into the paint. Give help if she needs it. Place the paint out of reach and have baby pat the paper to make hand prints and other smudges. Have baby's washcloth ready to wash the paint off before she tries to eat it. Hang her picture where she can see it. Make a handprint picture for baby's parents, too.

Baby can

- follow some easy directions

 in or out | 3–5 min | # 1 baby at a time

Materials and Notes
Blocks

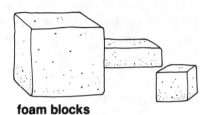

foam blocks

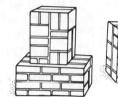

big cardboard blocks

soft blocks

dishpan of
two-inch cubes

same-size
stacking
blocks

unit blocks

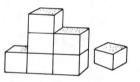

- If you use hard wooden blocks with baby, be sure to watch her carefully so that she doesn't bump on them and get hurt.
- Make sure blocks and their containers are safe and have no sharp edges.
- Make sure soft blocks and block coverings are made from colorfast, nontoxic materials.
- Make sure wooden colored blocks are nontoxic.
- Talk with parents about block activities that they can do with baby at home, such as putting blocks into a container for baby to dump out or having colorful, soft blocks for baby to play with.

Activity Checklist
Blocks

Block play for infants includes use of any materials that can be stacked—small colored cubes; wooden unit blocks; foam or cardboard blocks; homemade stacking toys, such as covered boxes. At the beginning, babies are given blocks to look at, hold, and drop. Later, older babies will learn to copy simple stacking games and use blocks for loading and unloading games.

Check for Each Age Group	*0–5 mo*	*5–9 mo*	*9–12 mo*
1. Some blocks are used daily (soft blocks for infants to hold, many different types of blocks for older babies to use).	—	—	—
2. Blocks are sorted and stored in an organized way (separated by shape and size, put on open shelves or in different boxes).	—	—	—
3. Blocks used are safe for children (nontoxic coverings, no sharp edges, large enough so they can't be swallowed, lightweight blocks for infants).	—	—	—
4. Adult talks to child about his block play (including how block looks, sounds, or feels; what he is doing with the blocks).	—	—	—
5. Blocks are accessible on low, open shelves or in other open storage for independent use by child.			—
6. Children can use blocks during morning and afternoon play times.			—

145

Talk About Block Building

When older babies or children are playing with <u>blocks</u>, place baby on your lap or in an infant seat where he can see what's going on. Talk to baby about what the other children are doing with the blocks.

Look. Barbara is stacking one block on another block. Oh! The blocks fell down!

Baby can

- watch moving things
- hear you talking

 in or out 1–3 min 1–2 babies

146

Roll the Block

Hold baby in your lap and roll a <u>large colored block</u> out in front of you. Try to use a block with a bell inside, to catch baby's attention. Talk to baby about the block, its color, the sound it makes, and how it moves.

There it goes. Watch the block roll, Beth! Can you hear the bell ring?

Baby can

- watch moving things

 in or out 1–5 min # 1 baby at a time

147

Block Mobile

Make a <u>mobile of lightweight blocks of different sizes and colors</u>. Use soft foam blocks, pop beads, textured cubes, or colored wooden beads. Small wooden blocks also work well if you drill a hole through the middle of them. Tie all blocks very tightly so that they won't fall. Hang the mobile where baby can watch it move.

Baby can

- watch moving things

 in or out 1–5 min # 1–2 babies

148

Holding Blocks

Prop each baby up with <u>pillows</u> in a <u>sturdy cardboard box</u>. Place several <u>colorful blocks</u> where baby can reach. Pick up a block to get baby's attention.

Here is a block. See the block?

Put the block into her hand. Soft blocks with a bell inside are good for getting baby interested. Allow baby to pick up and hold the blocks until she loses interest. Then try another toy or move baby to another area to play.

Baby can

- grasp a small thing
- sit with support

 in or out | 1–7 min | # 1–3 babies

149

Shape, Color and Texture Blocks

Place baby on her tummy on a <u>rug</u> or in a soft play area. Give her <u>blocks of different shapes</u>, <u>colors</u>, <u>and textures</u>. Foam shapes covered with different kinds of cloth are easy to make and safe.

Can you hold a block?

Place the block in baby's hand.

You're holding a soft red block.

Let baby reach out and grasp blocks until she loses interest.

Baby can

- lift head
- reach out when on stomach

 in or out | 3–10 min | # 1–6 babies

150

Knock Them Down

Place baby on her stomach on a <u>rug</u> or <u>blanket</u>. Stack a few <u>soft blocks</u> where baby can reach. Let her knock the blocks over. Tell her what she did.

Do you see the blocks? Look. I can stack them on top of each other. One, two, three.

Oh! Maribelle, you knocked them over!

Stack the blocks again for her. Then let her hold and play with the blocks.

Baby can

- reach out when on stomach

 in or out | 2–10 min | # 1–3 babies

151

Drop the Blocks

Place baby in a highchair. Put <u>colorful blocks</u> on his tray. Allow him to drop the blocks and look for them after they fall.

Did you drop the block, Mark? Where did it go?
It fell on the floor. There it is.

Take baby out of the highchair as soon as he is tired of this game. Later he can help you pick up the blocks by dropping them into a container, such as a dishpan.

Baby can

- drop things on purpose
- look for dropped things

 indoors | 3–5 min | # 1–4 babies

152

Blocks and Container

Fill a <u>plastic jar</u> with <u>2″ blocks</u>. Hand the jar to baby.

What's in the jar? Can you get some blocks out?
There's a red block. You got it out. Can you get another?

Place filled jars on low shelves where baby can reach. Make sure jars are refilled, either by you or as a game for an older baby.

Baby can

- take things out of a container

 in or out | 2–10 min | # 1–3 babies

153

Taking Blocks From the Shelf

Place five or six <u>large foam or cardboard blocks</u> for each baby on a low shelf. Help baby sit close to the shelf so that she can reach the blocks. Let her pull them from the shelf and move them around.

Those are big blocks, Nancy.
You can pick them up. You can push them.

Baby can

- move large lightweight things

 in or out | 1–10 min | # 1–2 babies

154

Jar Full of Blocks

Give baby an empty <u>plastic jar</u> and some <u>2″ colored blocks</u>. Help her drop a few blocks into the jar. Let her play with the jar and blocks and drop blocks into the jar when she wants.

There it goes, into the jar! Good girl, Evelyn!
Can you drop another one?

Keep two or three jars full of blocks on a low shelf, where babies can choose to play with them.

Baby can

- place things into a wide-mouth jar

 in or out   2–10 min   # 1–3 babies

155

Stacking Blocks

Sit with baby when he is playing with <u>large blocks</u>. Show him how to stack one block on top of another.

Look, Mario. I put one block on top of the other.
Can you put a block on top of this one?

See if he will copy what you did. Help him once or twice. If he is not interested, try again in a week or two. Later, try stacking smaller blocks with a baby who can stack large ones.

Baby can

- copy things you do

 in or out   2–5 min   # 1–3 babies

156

Dishpan Toys

Place <u>two dishpans</u> — <u>one with blocks</u>, the <u>other with toy cars or small people</u> — near baby. Let her play with the things in both containers at once in any way she wishes. When she starts to lose interest, help her put the blocks and toys back into the separate dishpans. Continue picking up with baby until she loses interest. Then quickly finish. Store the dishpans on low shelves, where babies can reach them.

Baby can

- place things in a container
- understand familiar words

 in or out   5–10 min   # 1–3 babies

Materials and Notes
Dramatic Play

toy tea set · puppets · pots and pans · toy telephone · unbreakable mirror · soft dolls · hats

- Be sure dolls, pocketbooks, kitchen toys, and other dramatic play materials have no chipped, loose, or broken pieces and are kept safe and in good repair.
- Make sure all mirrors have no sharp edges and are carefully secured. Special unbreakable mirrors are best.
- Ask parents to bring in unwanted hats, gloves, pocketbooks, kitchen items, or other dramatic play materials to use with babies.
- Talk with parents about how they can use dolls, pots, pans, big cooking utensils, old clothes, or other safe things found in the home for their baby's pretend play.

Activity Checklist
Dramatic Play

Dramatic play for infants includes simple experiences handling toys that they will later use to "make believe," such as dolls, stuffed animals, toy telephones, and pots and pans. The youngest infants try out these toys by grabbing, holding, dropping, and exploring them. They also join into play with adults. Later, toddlers will use these toys with adults or on their own to copy and act out what they see happening every day.

Check for Each Age Group	*0–5 mo*	*5–9 mo*	*9–12 mo*
1. Some dramatic play props are used daily (soft dolls and animals for the youngest infants; pots and pans, toy telephones, simple dress-ups, unbreakable mirrors, etc., for older infants).	—	—	—
2. Dramatic play materials are used indoors and outdoors.	—	—	—
3. Materials are stored in an organized way on low shelves where children can reach them (clothing is separated by kind; dishes and pots and pans are on shelves or in a box).	—	—	—
4. Dolls represent different races.	—	—	—
5. Dramatic play toys focus on what babies know and see in real life.	—	—	—
6. Adult talks to children as they explore and play with materials (gives words to what child is doing, names materials and relates them to real-life experiences).	—	—	—
7. Materials used are sturdy and safe for children (no small pieces, sharp edges, long scarves that could choke children, etc.).	—	—	—
8. Children are encouraged to use materials in their own way.	—	—	—
9. Adult pretends with child in play. Adult begins play so that child can copy or adds to play child has started (adult pretends to talk to child on toy telephone or pretends to eat from plate offered by child).		—	—

157

First Doll Play

Hold out a small, soft plastic <u>baby doll</u> for baby to grab and hold. Talk to him as he looks at it, moves it with his hand, and drops it.

That's a baby doll, Edward.
You're holding the baby doll.
It's soft, like you.
Do you want it again?

Baby can

- grasp and hold onto a small thing

 in or out | 1–5 min | **#** 1–3 babies

158

Watching Others Make Believe

Put <u>hats</u>, <u>dolls</u>, <u>pocketbooks</u>, and <u>an unbreakable tea set</u> on a low shelf or in a small dramatic play corner for older babies or toddlers to play with. Put a tiny baby in a safe place, where she can watch the activity with these toys. Try letting her watch as she snuggles on your lap, or put her in an infant seat, or prop her up with pillows in a box. Talk to her about what she sees.

What's Matthew doing, Sandy? He's holding a baby doll.
And look at Tonya. She has a hat on.

Baby can

- watch moving things
- sit with support

 indoors | 1–10 min | **#** 1–3 babies

159

Peek-a-boo With a Doll

Place baby on her tummy on a soft <u>rug</u> or blanket. Put a <u>doll</u> in front of her where she can reach.

See the doll. See the baby doll.
Let's cover her with the blanket.

Cover the doll with the blanket, then quickly take it off.

Where's the baby doll? Here's the doll!

If baby likes this game, do it again a few times.

Baby can

- play peek-a-boo

 in or out | 1–3 min | **#** 1–3 babies

Creative Activities

160

Baby can

- enjoy looking in a mirror

First Dress-Ups

Put an <u>unbreakable mirror</u> down low so that baby can see himself when he sits on the floor. Have two or three <u>hats</u> nearby so that you can put them on baby while he looks at his reflection. Use light hats and put them on baby for only a few seconds.

Look, Brian. There you are in the mirror!
See the hat? That's a hat with flowers.
Off it goes. Now you have on a different hat.
That's like the hat your daddy wears.

 in or out | 2–5 min | # 1–3 babies

161

Baby can

- copy some of your actions

Rock the Baby

Have baby sit with a <u>baby doll</u>. Show her how to cradle the baby in her arms and rock it. Help her rock the baby and chant or sing a little rocking song.

Sing "Rock-a-Bye Baby" or chant a little song of your own.

Rock the baby, Rock the baby,
Rock, rock, rock the baby.

Then see if she can rock the doll by herself. Enjoy her own special way of copying you.

 in or out | 1–5 min | # 1 baby at a time

162

Baby can

- copy some of your actions
- hold a toy

Using Pots and Pans

Put <u>lightweight pots</u>, <u>pans</u> and some <u>large plastic or wooden spoons</u> on a low shelf where baby can reach. Help baby sit near the shelf. Give him a spoon and show him how to stir. Then see if he can stir by himself. Let him explore the pots, pans, and spoons in many ways. Show him how to put tops on pots or to drop spoons into pans. Chant a little rhyme about stirring.

Stir, stir, stir. This is the way we stir.
We put the spoon into the pot and stir, stir, stir.

 in or out | 3–10 min | # 1–6 babies

163

Pictures of People Working

Cut out <u>magazine pictures of people doing different jobs</u>. <u>Paste</u> them onto <u>sturdy cardboard</u> and cover with <u>clear contact paper</u>. Show baby some of the pictures and point out a few things.

See the man? He's a farmer. See his hat?
Here's his dog. Here are his chickens.

Put some pictures in a box on a low shelf so that baby can take them out. She will look at and hold them in many ways and probably see how they taste, too.

Baby can

- pick up things
- look at pictures

 in or out | 1–10 min | # 1–6 babies

164

Toy Telephones

Place several <u>lightweight plastic telephones</u> on a low shelf where baby can reach. Show her how you hold the telephone and pretend to talk to someone. Give her a telephone and help her to hold the receiver to her ear. Make telephone ringing noises and talk to baby as she plays with the phone. Then let baby play with the telephone in her own way.

Ring, ring. Oh, the telephone is ringing.
Hello. It's for you, Anna.

Baby can

- copy some of your actions

 in or out | 1–3 min | # 1–3 babies

165

Dolls in a Bed

Put a few soft <u>baby dolls</u> in a <u>doll bed</u>. Show these to baby and let him play with them. Use the words "doll" and "doll bed" often as he plays.

What's this, Jeffrey? It's a doll.
Do you want the doll? You are holding the doll.
Pat the doll.
Here's the doll bed. The doll is in the doll bed.
Can you put your doll in the doll bed, too?

Baby can

- understand familiar words

 in or out | 3–10 min | # 1–4 babies

166

Baby can

- crawl while holding something
- remember where things are

Find the Dolls

Make sure the <u>dolls</u> are where baby has played with them before. Ask baby to show you where a doll is.

Where's the doll, Joan? Where's the doll?

If she can't find it, gently give her some help.

Here it is. Here is the doll.

If she does find it, talk with her about it.

You found the doll! It was in the doll bed.

 indoors | 3–10 min | **#** 1–2 babies

167

Baby can

- follow simple directions

Play With Dolls

When baby is playing with <u>dolls</u>, help her learn to rock, pat, hug, pick up, and hold the doll. Show her how you do these things. Then help her to do them. Name the things you and baby do with the dolls.

Do you like the doll, Mozelle?
Hug the doll. You do like that doll!
That's nice hugging.

 in or out | 2–10 min | **#** 1–3 babies

168

Baby can

- pay attention for a longer time

Watching Puppets

Put on a simple puppet show for baby. Use a <u>hand puppet</u> and make it do some simple things for baby to watch. Use a different voice as you make the puppet talk.

Hello. I am Woofy the dog. I like to sniff you.
Sniff, sniff, sniff. Did that tickle?

When you are done with your puppet show, let baby play with the puppet in his own way.

 in or out | 3–10 min | **#** 1–6 babies

169

Feeding Baby Dolls

Put some <u>clean</u>, <u>sturdy plastic bowls</u>, <u>cups</u>, and <u>big sturdy plastic spoons</u> into a <u>dishpan</u> with <u>two or three dolls</u>. Take out one doll. Show baby how you can pretend to feed the doll. See if baby will copy what to do. Then let baby play with the toys in his own way.

Did you feed the baby, Jimmy?
Oh! I see you're trying to feed yourself.

Baby can

- copy some actions

 in or out | 2–5 min | # 1–2 babies

170

Look in Pocketbooks

Choose a few safe things that you might find in a pocketbook for baby to play with. Try a <u>plastic change purse</u>, some <u>keys</u> on a key ring, a lightweight <u>comb</u> or <u>brush</u>, and some <u>tissues</u> baby can tear up. Put these into an old <u>pocketbook</u> without a snap or zipper. Place one pocketbook for each baby on a low shelf. Help baby find and play with the things in the pocketbook.

What's in the pocketbook, Sarah?
Oh! You found the keys.

Baby can

- explore things in a container

 indoors | 2–5 min | # 1–6 babies

171

Blankets and Pillows

Give each baby a <u>small blanket and pillow</u> to play with. Show her how to cover and uncover a <u>baby doll</u>.

It's time for baby to go to sleep.
Let's cover her up.

Then show her how you cover and uncover yourself. Put your head on the pillow. See if she can cover and uncover you.

Baby can

- copy some actions

 in or out | 3–5 min | # 1–6 babies

172

Find the Lost Doll

As baby watches, put a <u>doll</u> under a <u>box</u>, <u>dishpan</u>, <u>bowl or blanket</u>. Ask baby where the doll is. See if she will find the doll for you. Play again if baby likes the game. Pretend you don't know where the doll is. Show delight and surprise every time baby finds the doll.

Where's the doll, Krista? Where did she go?
Is she lost? Oh, you found her!
She was under the box.

Baby can

- find a hidden toy

 in or out   1–5 min # 1–2 babies

173

Many Different Dolls

Collect <u>many different safe dolls</u> for baby to play with. Put them all out in a row on a low open shelf. Call baby's attention to the dolls. Talk about the dolls she chooses to pull from the shelf.

That's a black girl doll, Sandra.
She has brown eyes.
Where is her nose? That's right!
Her nose is little, just like yours.
That doll is a boy doll. He has soft hair.

Baby can

- hold and play with a toy

 indoors   2–7 min # 1–3 babies

174

Mealtime Pretend Game

As you feed baby a snack or meal, pretend to have a taste of the <u>food</u> he is eating. Smile and make yummy food tasting noises as you pretend to taste. Then feed baby some more. See if he will join you in this fun by smiling, laughing or even offering you some of his <u>fingerfoods</u>. If he enjoys the game, play some more.

Yum, yum! These peaches are good.
I love these peaches. Yum, yum, yum!
Now you eat some, Davey.

Baby can

- eat some solid foods

 in or out ⊙ 1–3 min # 1–2 babies

Materials and Notes
Music

noise mobile

jingly toys

record player

pan with wooden spoons

jack-in-the-box

bells

chime apple

rattle

- Sing, hum, or chant to baby even if you don't think you have a musical voice. Babies listen much more closely to voices that move up and down.
- Be sure to turn the radio or record player off when you have finished a music activity. Too much noise in a room can be very distracting.
- Watch to make sure that babies who cannot move away from sounds enjoy what they hear. When they become fussy or bored, move them so that they can listen to something else.
- When you make your own mobiles or muscial toys, be sure to use things that are not too sharp, too heavy, or too small. Attach them very securely. Use them with extra care as baby gets his first teeth.
- You will find a list of songs and rhymes to use with the children at the end of this section. Share some of these songs with parents.

Activity Checklist
Music

Music for infants includes songs and chants, moving to rhythms, making music with musical toys or instruments, and listening to music made by others. At the beginning, babies enjoy gentle rhythmic movement, singing or chanting, and other soft music. Later, children want to move on their own and make their own sounds using everyday things and simple musical instruments.

Check for Each Age Group

	0–5 mo	5–9 mo	9–12 mo
1. Adult sings or chants daily to individual children.	—	—	—
2. Movement to music is included daily (baby held and rocked, toddler claps hands and dances).	—	—	—
3. Adult makes musical toys work for children and helps child work toy when able.	—	—	—
4. Adult avoids unnecessary background noise. Records, radio or tapes are on only when they are being used for children's activities.	—	—	—
5. Different types of music are used with children (special children's songs, classical records, music of different cultures). Music is played softly so that children can listen comfortably.	—	—	—
6. Adult helps make child aware of sounds by planning activities with sounds and talking about them.	—	—	—
7. Sound-making toys and musical instruments that children can use by themselves are accessible, such as wrist bells and mobiles to hit.	—	—	—
8. Adult makes songs personal by using children's names and by singing about daily events.	—	—	—

175

Watch and Listen

Hang a <u>musical crib toy or mobile</u> in a quiet area. Place baby in the area and make sure he can see the toy. Have the toy out of baby's reach but close enough to keep the baby's attention. A one-month-old can see best at about 12 inches. When baby is four months old, he should be able to see everything in a room. Wind up the toy or mobile. (Move baby when he loses interest.)

Listen, Paul. You are going to hear some music.
Listen. Do you hear the music?

Baby can

- turn head to sounds

 in or out | 2–10 min | # 1 or 2 babies

176

Sing to Baby

Hold baby close to you while you quietly hum or sing a favorite song. Try this activity while rocking, swaying, or walking with the child.

Do you like that song? I'm singing.

Sing again softly. You will find some songs you might sing at the end of this section. If you don't know the tunes, make up your own tunes to the words or chant the words in rhythm.

Baby can

- hear sounds

 in or out | 2–10 min | # 1–2 babies

177

Rock and Sing

Choose a simple song or chant to sing to baby. Rock to the movement of your voice. Try this while you sit with baby in your lap or carry baby around the room. If baby is very awake and ready to play, add a little bounce to your movement.

Baby, baby Michael.
I am holding Michael.

Baby can

- hear sounds

 in or out | ⊘ 2–10 min | # 1 or 2 babies

178

Listen to a Music Box

Place baby on a <u>rug</u> or soft area. Wind up a <u>music box toy</u> and place it on the floor close to her. Let baby listen. Sing along softly if you wish.

Do you want to hear some music? Listen, Tish.
Did you like that tune? Do you want to listen again?

Keep playing the music box until baby loses interest.

Baby can
- turn head to sounds

 in or out | 2 – 10 min | # 1 – 5 babies

179

Work Songs

Put baby in an <u>infant seat</u> close to you while you do your routine chores. As you wipe the table and put things away, sing to the child about what you are doing.

Mary is wiping the table.

Sing the same simple line over again several times.

Baby can
- hear sounds

 in or out | 2 – 5 min | # 1 – 4 babies

180

Dance With Baby

Dance around the room while you hold baby. This can be part of a daily routine, such as dancing over to the changing table, or you can make it a separate music activity. When you dance you can sing a <u>song</u> to baby or dance to music from a <u>music box or quiet record</u>.

Baby can
- hear sounds
- feel you move

 in or out | 1 – 3 min | # 1 baby at a time

181

Touching and Singing

Lay baby on her back on a soft <u>rug</u> or prop her up in a <u>sturdy box with pillows</u> in front of you. Sing songs that have you touch baby.

> *This little piggy went to market.*

Or try making up some songs of your own. Sing with a soft, simple chanting sound.

> *I'm going to get your nose.*

Gently creep your fingers from baby's toes up to her nose.

Baby can

- hear sounds

 in or out | 2–10 min | # 1–4 babies

182

Bouncy, Bouncy, Baby

Sit with baby on your lap and gently bounce your knees. While you bounce chant,

> *Bouncy, bouncy baby,*
> *up and down.*
> *Bouncy, bouncy baby,*
> *all around.*

Smile and laugh a lot with baby. See if she will begin to expect the bounce and almost bounce herself.

Baby can

- hear sounds

 in or out | 1–5 min | # 1–2 babies

183

Look and Find the Sound

Walk slowly around baby as you sing a favorite song. Help him to follow you and your voice. If she loses you, sing a little louder, stop, and say

> *Emma, I'm over here. Look around and find me.*

Sing different songs to baby this way and make a game of it.

Baby can

- turn head towards sounds

 in or out | 1–3 min | # 1–5 babies

184

Making Noise by Hitting at Things

Use <u>short strings</u> to tie some <u>noise-making toys</u> on a <u>rod or line</u>. Try jar lids, canning jar rings, plastic bells, or clacking wooden sticks. Place baby in an infant seat or on his back under the rod. Make sure he can reach the toys. Shake some of the things to get his attention and help him hit at them.

You hit the jar rings, Andy. Did you hear that noise?

Allow baby to play until he loses interest. Do not use this game with an older baby who can pull up on the line.

Baby can

- hit at things

 in or out | 1–10 min | # 1–3 babies

185

Listen to Wind Chimes

Hang <u>wind chimes</u> outdoors. Carry baby over to the wind chimes and gently move the chimes to make them ring. Hold baby so that she can see the chimes move.

Listen to the sounds the wind chimes make.
Isn't that pretty?

On a breezy day, place baby in a stroller or carriage where she can watch and listen. Try different kinds of wind chimes.

Baby can

- hear sounds
- look at moving things

 outdoors | 3–5 min | # 1–2 babies

186

Up and Down

Sit with baby in your lap facing you. Firmly hold his hands or arms and move baby back and forth from a lying down to a sitting up position while you chant or sing a song. Make lots of eye contact with baby and try to get him to make some sounds with you. Use the tune of "London Bridge is Falling Down."

Kevin's moving up and down,
up and down, up and down.
Kevin's moving up and down in my lap.

Baby can

- hear sounds
- begin to pull up

 in or out | 2–5 min | # 1 baby at a time

187

Music With Diapering

Put a <u>music box</u> in the diapering area where baby can see it. Let baby listen as you change her diapers. Music boxes with pull strings or on/off switches are good here. They take less time to start than wind-up ones.

Let's listen to the music box while I change your diaper.
Listen.
Do you see the music box? There it is!

Baby can

- turn head to sounds

 indoors   2–3 min   # 1 baby at a time

188

Finger Play Songs

Prop baby up in a <u>small sturdy box with pillows</u> or on a bean bag chair so that he can easily see you. Sit in front of him and sing <u>finger play songs</u> while you do the actions. Try "The Eensy Weensy Spider" or "Open, Shut Them."

Can you find my fingers? Watch me again, Theo.

Sing the song again for baby or go on to other songs.

Baby can

- hear sounds
- look around at things

 in or out   2–10 min   # 1–4 babies

189

Do What I Do

Help baby sit in an <u>infant seat</u> or prop her up in a <u>sturdy box with pillows</u>. Sit in front of her and sing. Use the tune of "Here We Go 'Round the Mulberry Bush." Clap your hands for baby to watch. Move baby's hands sometimes, too, and try other motions.

This is the way we clap our hands,
clap our hands, clap our hands.
This is the way we clap our hands
so early in the morning.

Baby can

- hear sounds
- watch things move

 in or out   1–10 min   # 1–6 babies

190

Kicking Game

Lay baby on her back on a soft <u>rug</u> or play area. Hold her feet and move them up and down as you chant.

> *Kick your feet up and down!*
> *Kick your feet my baby!*

Make a game out of this and see if baby will begin to kick her feet all by herself while you sing.

Baby can

- hear sounds
- move her feet

 in or out | 2–10 min | **#** 1–4 babies

191

Hold a Music Toy and Listen

Prop each baby up with <u>pillows</u> in a <u>sturdy box</u>. Choose a box that is big enough to hold baby and some toys, too. Wind up a <u>music toy</u> and put it into the box with baby.

> *Listen. Can you find the music? Here it is!*

Let baby look for or hold the toy while listening.

Baby can

- sit when supported
- hold a small toy

 in or out | 1–10 min | **#** 1–3 babies

192

Push a Toy for Sounds

Put baby on a <u>rug</u>. Place a <u>musical chime apple or ball</u> where baby can reach. Shake the toy.

> *Listen, Anita.*
> *Did you hear the chimes? Now you try.*

Help baby reach for the toy if she can't do it alone. Return the ball to her if it rolls away or use some large soft foam blocks to make a fence to stop the ball from rolling away.

Baby can

- lift head when on stomach
- hit or grasp

 in or out | 1–5 min | **#** 1 baby at a time

193

Ring a Bell

Place baby in an <u>infant seat</u> or prop him up on a <u>bean bag chair</u>. Place a <u>lightweight 3″ bell</u> in his hand. Show him how he can make the bell ring.

Here's a bell, Steven. Can you ring the bell?
Shake the bell. I hear the bell. It's ringing!
Good. Can you ring the bell again?

Try many kinds of plastic bells or bell rattles.

Baby can
- hold a rattle

 in or out | 2–5 min | # 1–3 babies

194

Routine Care Songs

Sing to baby about the things you do with her. The tune to "Here We Go 'Round the Mulberry Bush" works well for most things.

This is the way we change your diaper,
change your diaper, change your diaper . . .
This is the way we go outside,
go outside, go outside . . .

Sing songs about things you do with baby all through the day.

Baby can
- hear sounds

 in or out | 2–5 min | # 1–6 babies

195

Where Is the Toy?

Place baby on <u>rug</u> or soft play area. Sit in front of her where she can watch you. Place a <u>toy</u> in front of her and cover a part of it with a <u>small cloth</u>. Sing to the tune of "Where is Thumbkin."

Where is the ball?

If baby uncovers the toy, sing *There it is!*

If not, finish the song and uncover it yourself singing *There it is. I found it.*

Baby can
- hear sounds
- look at things around her

 in or out | 2–5 min | # 1–4 babies

196

Bang to a Song

While baby is sitting in his highchair, give him <u>one or two blocks or spoons</u> to bang on his tray. Sing the song "This Old Man" and bang baby's tray gently for him to copy as you sing

Nick-nack paddy-whack

Baby can

- sit in a highchair
- bang things

 indoors | 2 – 10 min | # 1 – 5 babies

197

Bang Things and Listen

While baby is waiting to be fed, place <u>safe sound-making toys</u> such as big plastic cooking spoons, plastic cups, or rattles on her table or tray. Choose two that will make different sounds as she plays.

Can you make music with these? I hear you banging the big spoon. It goes clank, clank, clank.

Now you are hitting with the keys? That's right. They go click, click, click.

Baby can

- play with things by banging them

 indoors | 2 – 10 min | # 1 – 3 babies

198

Baby's Sounds

When you are with baby and she starts to coo or babble, choose a sound she makes and sing it back to her softly.

I heard you, Katerina.
Ba, ba, ba, ba, ba, ba!

Do this as often as you like at any time of the day. Be sure to look into baby's eyes as you copy her sounds.

Baby can

- hear sounds
- make a few cooing sounds

 in or out | 2 – 5 min | # 1 – 3 babies

199

Baby can

- hear sounds
- look around at things

Peek and Sing

Help baby sit outside in a safe, comfortable place. Move in front of baby where she can easily see you. Hide your face behind your hands and sing a peek-a-boo game.

Peek-a-boo. I see you!
Can you find me now?

Move back and forth so baby can watch you hide and come back.

 outdoors | 2–10 min | # 1–4 babies

200

Baby can

- hold and shake toys

Choose a Music Toy

Place some <u>sound toys</u> such as shakers, bells, rattles, and clackers on a low shelf. Have baby sit or lie on his tummy where he can reach toys. As he chooses a toy from the shelf, name the toy for him and say the sound the toy makes.

Which music toy are you going to play with?
I see. You are holding the bell.
The bell goes ding, ding, ding.

Have more than one of the most popular toys on the shelf.

 indoors | 1–20 min | # 1–6 babies

201

Baby can

- hold and bang a toy on purpose
- copy some actions

Play a Xylophone

Place several <u>xylophones</u> on a low shelf for baby to choose.

Do you want to play a xylophone? Watch me.

Show baby how to hit the instrument to make noise. Help him try to play the xylophone.

You can do it too, Andrew.

Try to sing the notes he plays.

 indoors | 2–10 min | # 1–3 babies

202

Moving to Music

Sit or kneel in front of baby. Hold him under his arms and pull him up so that he is standing. Turn on <u>a music box or active record</u> and begin to move your body up and down or back and forth to the music. Encourage baby to copy your actions and move along with the music.

Oh. Look at you bounce.
You're dancing to the music.

Baby can

- bounce on his feet with support

🏠 in or out | 🕐 1–5 min | # 1 baby at a time

203

Listen to Sounds and Their Names

When baby is banging a <u>toy</u>, <u>cup</u>, <u>or spoon</u> to make noise, repeat the sounds she makes or name the sounds with words.

Bang, bang, bang. I heard you hitting that spoon, Jinsy.
Bang, bang, bang, bang, bang. You are making more sounds with that spoon. What nice music!

Baby can

- make noise with toys on purpose

🏠 in or out | 🕐 1–3 min | # 1 baby at a time

204

Action Songs

Sit with baby on a <u>rug</u>. Sing <u>finger-play songs</u> with him. Hold his hands or feet and move his body to the actions of the songs. Try songs such as "The Eensy Weensy Spider," "This Little Piggy," or "Pat-a-Cake."

Try other action songs you will find at the end of this section.

Baby can

- hear sounds
- begin to sit

🏠 in or out | 🕐 2–15 min | # 1–3 babies

205

Ring Around the Rosy

Hold baby in your arms and sing "Ring Around the Rosy."

Ring around the rosy,
A pocket full of posies,
Ashes, ashes,
We all fall down.

When you sing "We all fall down," bend over or stoop low so that baby feels the movement of the song and its action.

Baby can

- hear sounds
- feel movement

 in or out | 2–5 min | # 1–2 babies

206

Rolling to Music

Fold a <u>blanket or large towel</u> in half and roll it tightly into a log-shaped cushion. Lay baby on his tummy over the cushion and gently roll him a little bit back and forth as you sing or chant a familiar song or play a <u>soft record</u>.

Rock-a-bye, rock-a-bye, rock-a-bye, my baby.

Baby can

- lift head and chest while on tummy

 indoors | 1–10 min | # 1 baby at a time

207

Pull or Shake for Sounds

Securely hang <u>two or three musical toys</u> from a sturdy shelf or window sill so that baby can pull or shake different strings to make different musical toys work. Music boxes with pullstrings, a bell, or canning jar rings work well. Make sure strings are short and far enough apart so that baby can't get caught in them. Show him how to pull or shake the strings to make music.

Can you pull on the string? Good, Arthur.
Now listen. Pull another string.

Baby can

- grab, pull

 indoors | 2–10 min | # 1–2 babies at a time

Creative Activities

208

Singing About Toys

When baby is sitting in his highchair waiting to be fed, give him <u>one or two small toys</u> to play with. When he picks one up sing a little song to the tune of "London Bridge is Falling Down."

Tommy has a little bear, little bear, little bear.
Tommy has a little bear in his hand.

Change this song for different toys, or try using the names of foods baby eats.

Baby can
- hear sounds
- pick up small things

 in or out   2–5 min # 1–3 babies

209

Pat Pat Pat

Bring out <u>old pots and pans</u> or anything else that will make a good noise when baby beats on it. Put on an active record and sing a happy song. Pat baby's pan to the beat of the music. Encourage baby to pat along with you.

Pat, pat, pat the drum.

Baby can
- bang to make a noise

 in or out   2–10 min # 1–4 babies

210

Where Is Baby?

While sitting with a small group of babies, choose someone's name and sing to the tune of "Where is Thumbkin?"

Where is Wendy?

Point to the child and say

There she is. This is Wendy.

Play this game using the names of children and adults in the room.

Baby can
- look around at different people

 in or out 2–10 min # 1–5 babies

211

Crawl to Music Toys

Make a little area where <u>music toys</u> are stored on a low shelf. Allow baby to crawl to this place and choose toys to use. Remind her that these toys are in this place.

Look. Do you want to make some music?
Here are some bells you can ring.
Come over here, Carrie.

Try to have more than one of each popular music toy.

Baby can

- grab, grasp pull, let go

 indoors | 1–10 min | # 1–6 babies

212

Play a Toy Piano

Place a child's <u>toy piano</u> where baby can reach it.

Can you play the piano?

Show her how to make sounds by pressing the keys. She will probably use her whole hand at first and hit many notes at once. Help her hit one key with one finger. Let her play while you sing or hum the sounds she makes. Talk about them with her.

Boom. You played loudly, didn't you?
Bing. That was a high sound!

Baby can

- use a pointing finger to touch

 indoors | 2–7 min | # 1 baby at a time

213

Sing Together

Sing a simple tune to baby using a sound you know he can make. Smile and put lots of expression into your sounds. See if baby will start to sing the song with you and begin to make the sound you are making. Show him how happy you are with any sounds he makes.

Good singing. I like your song, Eddy.
Want to sing it again?

Baby can

- copy a few sounds

 in or out | 2–10 min | # 1–3 babies

214

So Big

Sit with baby on a soft <u>rug</u> or play area. Chant or sing *How big is Marty? Sooo big.*

As you sing the word *Sooo,* make your voice change to a higher pitch and raise your arms for baby to copy. If he doesn't copy you, help him by lifting his arms.

Baby can

- copy simple arm movements

 in or out | 2–5 min | # 1–2 babies

215

Drop Things to Hear Different Sounds

Place <u>three different containers</u> together where baby can reach. Try containers of metal, plastic, wood, or cardboard. Give baby <u>different things to drop</u> into the containers (a bell, block, spoon, etc.). Make sure the things are too large to swallow.

Drop this block in here. Clunk. Did you hear that? Now drop the bell. Ring. Now try it in the plastic container.

Baby can play with this on his own. Try fastening the containers to a low shelf or board and keep things for dropping nearby.

Baby can

- drop things into a container
- follow simple directions

 in or out | 2–5 min | # 1–2 babies

216

Pat-A-Cake

Play pat-a-cake with baby. Try to get him to make some sounds while you chant the song. Help him to do the motions along with you. When you are finished smile, clap your hands, and hug baby.

Yea! We sang a song. Let's sing it again.

Baby can

- copy a few sounds and actions

 in or out | 2–10 min | # 1–3 babies

217

Baby can

- copy simple arm movements

Pop!

Sit baby on a <u>blanket</u> outside. Sit down in front of him with a <u>jack-in-the-box</u> in your lap. Wind the Jack-in-the-box so that the music plays for baby. Then when Jack pops out, throw both your hands high in the air and say *Pop!* See if baby will copy all your actions and move along with the music.

 in or out 2–10 min # 1–4 babies

218

Baby can

- copy a few simple actions

This Is the Way

Seat baby in front of a <u>big mirror</u> so that she can see herself. Sit behind her and start to sing about her eyes, nose, mouth, and hair to the tune of "Here We Go 'Round the Mulberry Bush."

This is the way we touch our nose . . .

Pat your nose and see if baby will copy you. If she doesn't, help her move her hand so that she pats her nose while you sing. Sing the song a few more times and change the body part each time.

 indoors 2–10 min # 1–6 babies

219

Baby can

- copy a few simple actions

Open, Shut Them

While baby is in a highchair waiting to be fed, chant or sing the song "Open, Shut them." You will find the words at the end of this section. Hold your hands in front of baby so that he can watch while you sing. Try to get him to copy your hand movements. Sing the song several times and each time creep your fingers up baby to tickle his chin.

Did that tickle, Will?
You liked that song.

 indoors 2–4 min # 1–6 babies

220

Baby can

- follow simple directions
- understand some words

Find and Play the Music Toy

Have <u>music toys</u> on a low shelf where baby can reach. Help her to find toys that you name.

Let's play some music. Trudy, you go get the bells.
Here they are. Good. You found the bells.
Play the bells.
Shawn, you go get the drum. Play the drum.

Try this outdoors. Put the toys in a musical instrument box and make music outdoors.

 in or out | 1–10 min | # 1–6 babies

221

Baby can

- follow simple directions
- understand some words

Singing and Crawling

Look around for a <u>familiar toy</u>, such as a toy car, and tell baby you want to get it. Point to the toy so that baby knows where it is. Sing to the tune of "London Bridge is Falling Down."

We are going to get the car,
  get the car, get the car.
We are going to get the car,
  get the car right now.

Crawl over to the toy while singing. Play again with a block.

 in or out | 2–10 min | # 1–6 babies

222

Baby can

- copy simple actions

Rocking Your Knees

Put baby up on his hands and knees and kneel beside him on your hands and knees. Play an <u>active record</u> or sing a happy song. Rock back and forth on your knees to the music and try to get baby to rock with you. If baby likes this, try other movements while kneeling, such as shaking your head or crawling to the music.

 in or out | 1–10 min | # 1–6 babies

223

Baby can

- push or roll toys

Roll the Toy

Sit with baby in a play area with a <u>few toys</u>. Roll a ball or toy to baby while you sing to the tune of "Row, Row, Row Your Boat."

Roll, roll, roll the car. Roll it to my baby.
Roll it back, roll it back, roll it back to me.

Roll the toy back and forth with the baby several more times. Baby may play longer if you change the toys you are rolling.

 in or out | 2–10 min | # 1–3 babies

224

Baby can

- roll a ball or push toy

This Is the Way We Roll the Ball

Sit with baby on a <u>big blanket</u>. Roll a <u>ball</u> to her and see if she will roll it back to you. While you play this game sing to the tune of "Here We Go 'Round the Mulberry Bush."

This is the way we roll the ball . . .

See if baby will sing along with you.

 in or out | 2–10 min | # 1–5 babies

225

Baby can

- look at pictures in books
- copy a few simple actions

Music and Pictures

Choose a <u>book with good</u>, <u>clear pictures</u>. Sit with baby. Find a picture and name what you see for baby. Then tap the picture while you chant to the tune of "Clap Your Hands."

Tap, tap, tap the cat.
Tap the cat right now.

Continue on through the book and sing a song for other pictures you name. Help baby tap the picture, too, and then see if he will do it by himself.

 in or out | 1–5 min | # 1–2 babies

226

Peek-A-Boo With a Musical Instrument

Put <u>three or four different sounding musical instruments</u> into a <u>big box</u> (a xylophone, a bell, some clacking sticks, a drum). Have baby listen as you play one instrument in the box. Don't let him see what you're playing.

Do you hear that sound? What is it?

Take the instrument from the box and play it again.

Hear it? It's the xylophone! Listen!

Baby can

- pay attention for a longer time

 in or out | 2–7 min | # 1–6 babies

227

Old MacDonald

Find <u>several stuffed animals</u> that are familiar to baby and sing "Old MacDonald." When you get to the animal's name or sound, hold up the stuffed toy and see if baby will sing the name or make the sound with you. You may want to start out with only one or two animals at first and then add more later.

With a meow, meow here, meow, meow there,
Here a meow, there a meow, everywhere a meow,
meow . . .

Baby can

- know a few animals and their sounds

 in or out | 2–10 min | # 1–6 babies

228

Shake Things to Hear Different Sounds

Gather <u>a few musical instruments</u>, <u>one set for you and one for baby</u>. Try two rattles and two drums, or two bells and two clacking rattles. Shake the toys and sing to the tune of "Here We Go 'Round the Mulberry Bush." Help baby copy you.

This is the way we shake the rattle,
shake the rattle, shake the rattle.
This is the way we shake the rattle
so early in the morning.

Baby can

- copy what you do

 in or out | 2–5 min | # 1–2 babies

Songs and Rhymes

A Hunting We Will Go

A hunting we will go, a hunting we will go.
Hi-ho the merrio, a hunting we will go.

Clap, Clap, Clap Your Hands

Clap, clap,   clap your hands,
Clap your hands together.
Clap, clap,   clap your hands,
Clap your hands right now.
Additional verses: (2) Touch your nose   (3) Tap your knees
(4) Pat your head

Did You Ever See a Lassie (or Laddie)

Did you ever see a lassie, a lassie, a lassie?
Did you ever see a lassie go this way and that?
Go this way and that way, go this way and that way.
Did you ever see a lassie go this way and that?

Eensy Weensy Spider

The eensy weensy spider went up the water spout.
Down came the rain and washed the spider out.
Out came the sun and dried up all the rain;
And the eensy weensy spider went up the spout again.

Head and Shoulders, Knees and Toes

Head and shoulders, knees and toes, knees and toes.
Head and shoulders, knees and toes, knees and toes.
Eyes and ears and mouth and nose.
Head and shoulders, knees and toes, knees and toes.

Here We Go 'Round the Mulberry Bush

Here we go 'round the mulberry bush, the mulberry bush, the
mulberry bush,
Here we go 'round the mulberry bush, so early in the morning.

Hey Diddle Diddle

Hey diddle diddle the cat and the fiddle.
The cow jumped over the moon.
The little dog laughed to see such fun,
And the dish ran away with the spoon.

Hickory Dickory Dock

Hickory, dickory, dock! The mouse ran up the clock.
The clock struck one, the mouse ran down! Hickory, dickory dock!

I Am Walking

I am walking, walking, walking, I am walking, walking, walking,
I am walking, walking, walking, I am walking, walking, walking,
Now I stop.

Hush Little Baby

Hush, little baby, don't say a word, Momma's gonna buy you a mocking bird.
If that mocking bird won't sing, Momma's gonna buy you a diamond ring.
If that diamond ring turns brass, Momma's gonna buy you a looking glass.
If that looking glass gets broke, Momma's gonna buy you a billy goat.
If that billy goat won't pull, Momma's gonna buy you a cart and bull.
If that cart and bull turn over, Momma's gonna buy you a dog named Rover.
If that dog named Rover, won't bark, Momma's gonna buy you a horse and cart.
If that horse and cart fall down, you'll still be the sweetest little baby in town.

If You're Happy and You Know It

If you're happy and you know it, clap your hands (clap, clap)
If you're happy and you know it, clap your hands (clap, clap)
If you're happy and you know it then your face will surely show it.
If you're happy and you know it, clap your hands. (clap, clap)
Additional verses: (2) Stamp your feet (3) Nod your head (4) Pat your knees (5) Wave good-bye

I'm A Little Teapot

I'm a little teapot short and stout.
Here is my handle, here is my spout.
When I get all steamed up, hear me shout,
"Just tip me over and pour me out."

Jack and Jill

Jack and Jill went up the hill to fetch a pail of water.
Jack fell down and broke his crown and Jill came tumbling after.

Jack Be Nimble

Jack be nimble.
Jack be quick.
Jack jumped over the candlestick.

Lazy Mary

Lazy Mary will you get up, will you get up, will you get up?
Lazy Mary will you get up, will you get up this morning.

Little Green Frog

Ah—ump went the little green frog one day.
Ah—ump went the little green frog.
Ah—ump went the little green frog one day
And his eyes went blink, blink, blink.

Little Jack Horner

Little Jack Horner sat in a corner
Eating his Christmas pie.
He stuck in his thumb and pulled out a plum
And said, "What a good boy am I."

London Bridge

London bridge is falling down, falling down, falling down,
London bridge is falling down, my fair lady.

Muffin Man

Do you know the muffin man, the muffin man, the muffin man?
Do you know the muffin man who lives on Drury Lane?

Oats, Peas, Beans

Oats, peas, beans and barley grow;
Oats, peas, beans and barley grow;
Do you or I or anyone know
How oats, peas, beans and barley grow?

One Little, Two Little, Three Little Babies

One little, two little, three little babies,
Four little, five little, six little babies,
Seven little, eight little, nine little babies,
Ten little babies I know!

One, Two, Buckle Your Shoe

One, two, buckle your shoe.
Three, four, shut the door.
Five, six, pick up sticks.
Seven, eight, lay them straight.
Nine, ten, a big fat hen!

Open, Shut Them

Open, shut them, open, shut them, give a little clap.
Open, shut them, open, shut them, lay them in your lap.
Creep them, creep them, creep them, creep them right up to your chin.
Open wide your little mouth, but do not let them in.

Pat-A-Cake

Pat-a-cake, pat-a-cake, baker's man,
Bake me a cake as fast as you can.
Pat it and prick it and mark it with a B,
And put it in the oven for baby and me.

Pop Goes the Weasel

All around the carpenter's bench
The monkey chased the weasel.
The monkey thought 'twas all in fun.
Pop! Goes the weasel.

Peas Porridge Hot

Peas porridge hot, peas porridge cold,
Peas porridge in the pot, nine days old.
Some like it hot, some like it cold,
Some like it in the pot nine days old.

Ring Around the Rosy

Ring around the rosy,
A pocket full of posies.
Ashes, ashes,
We all fall down.

Rock-A-Bye Baby

Rock-a-bye baby, on the tree top,
When the wind blows, the cradle will rock,
When the bough breaks, the cradle will fall.
And down will come baby, cradle and all.

Sing A Song of Sixpence

Sing a song of sixpence, a pocket full of rye.
Four and twenty blackbirds baked in a pie.
When the pie was opened the birds began to sing,
Wasn't that a dainty dish to set before the king?

Teddy Bear

Teddy bear, teddy bear, turn around.
Teddy bear, teddy bear, touch the ground,
Teddy bear, teddy bear, show your shoe,
Teddy bear, teddy bear, that will do!

There Was a Duke of York

There was a Duke of York.
He had ten thousand men.
He marched them up the hill.
And then he marched them down again.

When you're up, you're up.
And when you're down, you're down.
And when you're only half way up
You're neither up nor down.

This is the Way

This is the way we put on our pants, put on our pants, put on our pants.
This is the way we put on our pants, so early in the morning.

This Little Piggy

This little piggy went to market and this little piggy stayed home,
This little piggy had roast beef and this little piggy had none,
And this little piggy went, "Wee, wee, wee, wee," all the way home.

This Old Man

This old man, he played one,
He played nick-nack on my thumb,
With a nick-nack paddy-whack, give a dog a bone,
This old man came rolling home.
Additional verses: (2) Shoe; (3) Knee; (4) Door; (5) Hive;
(6) Sticks; (7) Up in heaven; (8) Gate; (9) Spine; (10) Once again

Twinkle, Twinkle, Little Star

Twinkle, twinkle, little star, how I wonder what you are.
Up above the world so high, like a diamond in the sky,
Twinkle, twinkle, little star, how I wonder what you are.

Two Little Blackbirds

Two little blackbirds sitting on a hill.
One named Jack and one named Jill.
Fly away Jack, fly away Jill.
Come back Jack, come back Jill.
Two little blackbirds sitting on a hill.
One named Jack and one named Jill.

Wheels on the Bus

The wheels on the bus go round and round,
Round and round, round and round.
The wheels on the bus go round and round
All through the town.
Additional verses: (2) Baby goes wah wah wah (3) Lights go blink,
blink, blink (4) Driver says move on back (5) Money goes clink,
clink, clink (6) People go up and down (7) Wipers go swish, swish,
swish

Where Is Thumbkin

Where is thumbkin? Where is thumbkin?
Here I am, here I am.
How are you today sir? Very well I thank you.
Run and play, run and play.

Where Oh Where Is Pretty Little Susie?

Where oh where is pretty little Susie?
Where oh where is pretty little Susie?
Where oh where is pretty little Susie?
Way down yonder in the pawpaw patch.

Yankee Doodle

Oh Yankee Doodle went to town a-riding on a pony,
He stuck a feather in his cap and called it macaroni.
Yankee Doodle keep it up; Yankee Doodle Dandy,
Mind the music and the step and with the girls be handy.

Your Own Creative Activities

Write your own activities on these two pages. You will find more information on writing your own activities in the Planning section, pages 12–13.

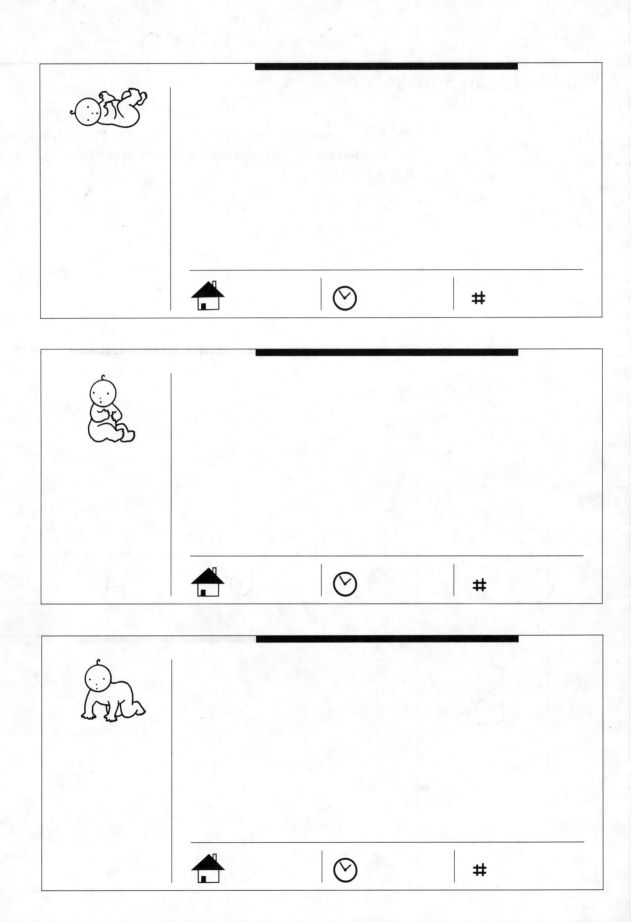

Activities for Learning
from the World Around
Them

Index

*of Activities for Learning from the
World Around Them*

*R*eal things in the world around us are fun to watch and learn about. They move, disappear, change, and are always surprising because they do things on their own. Being outside where there is so much to see and feel often helps to calm you and the babies. Good early experiences outdoors can help a child gain an interest in nature. Early activities outdoors can also help a child feel safe in rougher, more natural places.

The senses — how we hear, see, smell, taste, and feel — are our main ways of experiencing the world throughout our lives. As babies grow, they need to learn ways to understand all the information coming in through their senses. They form ideas to help them understand things in the world around them. One idea babies learn in their first year of life is that something may look like it is gone but really may only be out of sight. Games like peek-a-boo and hiding toys under a blanket help babies form this idea. Other ideas about number, shape, size, and color come gradually throughout the preschool years. Starting very early in life, a child needs many real experiences as a basis for these ideas. They also need adults who talk to them and describe what they see, hear, and feel.

In this section there are many activities to help infants use their senses and learn about the world around them. There are also activities that give babies a chance to find hidden toys or play with things of different shape, size, and color. These activities will help you teach babies some of what they will need in order to become good thinkers.

Materials and Notes
Nature

sand and water toys

animal toys

nature mobiles

aquarium

- Try to take baby outside every day. Use strollers or baby carriages for walks. Bring blankets out on nice days. When the weather is bad, go out for a shorter time when the weather lets up, but do go out.
- Dress baby properly for the weather.
- On hot days, make sure baby has plenty to drink. Find shady places for baby to play.
- Check to make sure that no plants around baby, indoors or out, are poisonous.
- Check outdoor areas for things that might hurt baby. Look for small or sharp things, insects, animal droppings, or trash. Keep babies safe from older, more active children, too.

Activity Checklist
Nature

Nature for infants includes experiences in exploring natural things both indoors and out, learning words for natural things, and beginning what can be a lifelong appreciation and respect for nature. For the youngest babies, a daily walk in a stroller or being held up to look out the window is a nature experience. Later, babies will enjoy picking up and inspecting many natural things or looking at nature picture books.

Check for Each Age Group	*0–5 mo*	*5–9 mo*	*9–12 mo*
1. Children have a daily outdoor time, weather permitting.	—	—	—
2. Adult regularly points out to children natural outdoor things, such as flowers, birds, insects, plants, animals.	—	—	—
3. Adult often names and talks about natural things with children.	—	—	—
4. Some natural things are displayed safely indoors.	—	—	—
5. Pictures and picture books of familiar natural things are often displayed where children can see and touch them.	—	—	—
6. Adult encourages children to explore safe, natural things with their senses.	—	—	—
7. Adult shows appreciation and respect for nature when with children (shows curiosity and interest rather than disgust about insects, spider webs, worms; has positive attitude about going outside in different kinds of weather; etc.).	—	—	—
8. Adult asks children easy questions about natural things.		—	—

229

Take a Walk

Take baby outside in a <u>stroller</u>, <u>baby carriage</u>, <u>or baby carrier</u>. Take a little walk around the yard or neighborhood and talk to baby about what both of you see, smell, feel, and hear.

Did you hear the bird? Tweet, tweet.

Try walks on hot, mild, cool, and cold days.
Try walks on sunny, cloudy, bright, or gray days.

Baby can

- sit supported
- look at things

 outdoors | 10–30 min | # 1–3 babies

230

Watch Things Blow in the Wind

On a mild, breezy day find a place where baby can watch things move in the wind. Try under a tree with leaves rustling; near a bush with leaves moving; or next to long, swaying grass. Put baby on her back on a <u>soft blanket</u> or in an <u>infant seat</u> so that she can watch the changing patterns.

Those leaves are moving, Kelisha.
The wind is blowing them.

Baby can

- look at moving things

 outdoors | 1–10 min | # 1–6 babies

231

Feeling Grass

On a mild day, put a <u>blanket</u> on the grass. Place baby near the edge of the blanket so that he can reach out for the grass. Pat the grass and let him try to reach and feel it. When he touches the grass, tell him about what he is doing.

That's grass, Teddy. Can you feel it?
Pat the grass. It's all green, isn't it?

Baby can

- lift head and reach out when on stomach

 outdoors | 3–15 min | # 1–6 babies

232

Hit at a Nature Mobile

Securely tie <u>seashells</u>, <u>sturdy twigs</u>, <u>feathers</u>, or <u>other interesting outdoor things</u> to a <u>rod</u>. Make sure the things are not sharp or harmful to baby. Place each baby under a rod in an <u>infant seat</u> or on a soft <u>rug</u>. Let baby look and hit at the things. Tell him what he is doing.

You hit a seashell. It went clack against the other seashell, didn't it, Ho?

Baby can

- hit at things

 indoors | 2–10 min | # 1–3 babies

233

Pretty Leaf Mobile

Put pretty, bright <u>fall leaves</u> between two pieces of <u>clear contact paper</u>. Hang them from a <u>rod</u> or <u>mobile</u> where baby can see them. Make sure she can see the flat side of the leaf, not just the thin edge. Use one mobile for each baby.

Aren't these pretty leaves?
Here's a red one, and here's a yellow one.

Leaves can also be ironed between two pieces of wax paper. Cover the wax paper with paper towels while you iron.

Baby can

- look at moving things

 indoors | 2–10 min | # 1–3 babies

234

Watching the Sunshine Sparkle

Cover some <u>cardboard shapes</u> with <u>aluminum foil</u>. Hang them from a <u>dowel or hanger</u> in a sunny window where they will shine in the sunlight. Place or hold baby so that she can watch. Open the window to let a breeze gently move the shiny shapes. Try hanging the mobile outside. Put baby in an infant seat or bean bag chair near enough to watch.

Look at the shiny circle, Deirdre.
See it sparkle in the sun?

Baby can

- look at things

 in or out | 2–10 min | # 1–4 babies

235

Hold Toy Animals

Put each baby into a <u>sturdy box</u> and prop her up with <u>pillows</u>. Place a few cuddly or soft plastic <u>toy animals</u> in the box where she can reach. Talk about each animal as you put it near her.

Look, Evie. Here's a kitten.
Can you hold the kitten?
And here's a dog. He's soft.

Baby can

- sit supported
- pick up a small toy

 in or out   2–15 min   # 1–3 babies

236

Watching Rain or Snow

On a rainy or snowy day, hold baby in your arms or put him in an <u>infant seat</u> so that he can watch out a window. Tap the window to get his attention and talk about what he sees.

See the rain? It makes shiny drops on the window.
It's wet outside, and we are so warm and dry in here.

If he is interested, let him watch some more.

Baby can

- sit supported

 indoors   1–10 min   # 1–2 babies

237

Splashing in Water

Fill a <u>baby pool or tub</u> with 1/8 inch of <u>warm water</u>. Gently lay baby on her back in the pool. Make sure the water is so shallow that it doesn't even come up to her ears. If baby is happy in the water, help her pat the water with her arms and legs. If she seems timid or afraid, soothe her or take her out.

Do you like that water? It's wet and warm.

Take baby out, dry, and cuddle her before she becomes cold or fussy. Never leave baby alone in the water.

Baby can

- move arms and legs

 in or out   5–15 min   # 1–3 babies

238

Watching Pets

Set up a pet area in the room out of baby's reach. Put <u>goldfish</u>, <u>gerbils</u>, <u>or hamsters</u> in a sturdy <u>aquarium tank</u>. Place baby near the tank on a <u>blanket</u>, in a <u>stroller</u>, or <u>infant seat</u> to watch. If you have gerbils or hamsters, make sure they are active when you put baby near. If he doesn't look, try turning his attention to the tank by snapping your fingers or tapping lightly on the glass.

Look, Thomas. Do you see the goldfish?
They're swimming in the water.

Baby can

- watch moving things

 indoors 1–10 min # 1–2 babies

239

Bouncing on Grass

When babies are playing outside on a <u>blanket</u> hold one baby up in sand or grass so that he can feel how it tickles his feet. Let him bounce up and down as you hold him. Laugh with him and sing a little song you make up.

Bouncy, bouncy, bouncy.
Little Joey is bouncing.
Bouncing in the grass!

Baby can

- bounce when held in a standing position

 outdoors 1–2 min # 1 baby at a time

240

Bird Watching

Put a <u>bird feeder</u> outside a low window. Keep it filled with <u>sunflower seeds</u>. When birds come to feed, pick up baby and show her the birds. If you have a low windowsill put her down and see if she will pull up to look.

See the birds, Tina? There's one!
He's eating the seed.
Oh! He flew away.

Or watch with baby from a rocking chair near the window.

Baby can

- pull to a standing position

 indoors 2–10 min # 1–3 babies

241

Reaching for Toy Animals

Put a selection of <u>toy animals</u> on a low shelf where baby can reach. Place baby near the shelf and let him choose animals to play with. Tell baby what sounds the animals make.

Nicky, see the animal toys?
You picked up a cow.
The cow says moooo!

Try taking a box of animals outside for baby to play with, too.

Baby can

- pick up a toy

 in or out | 1–15 min | # 1–6 babies

242

Weather Talk

Look out the window with baby. If the window is low enough, help baby pull up to stand so that she can see. Talk about what the weather is like.

It's so cold outside today. Let's bundle up when we go out.

When you go out with baby, talk about the weather some more.

Brrrr! Isn't it cold? I'm glad we wore our mittens.

Baby can

- pull to a standing
  position

 in or out | 1–3 min | # 1–3 babies

243

Getting Ready to Go Outside

As you get ready to go outside, talk about what you are doing and what you will see.

We're going outside now.
We will see flowers and trees and grass.

When you are outside, point out the things you talked about.

Look. Here's a flower. It's a pretty flower.

Baby can

- look and listen

 in or out | 2–10 min | # 1–5 babies

244

Baby can

- feel and see
- coo to show delight

Feather or Leaf Tickle

Securely tie together a few <u>clean fresh leaves or feathers</u> with a <u>string</u>. Hang these near the changing table where baby can see them. While changing baby, take them down and use them to gently tickle his arms, legs, tummy, and feet.

Does that feather tickle, Brian?
I'm tickling your toes.

When outside, gently tickle baby with leaves or grass.

 in or out | 1–2 min | # 1 baby at a time

245

Baby can

- pick things up

Water Play With Toys

On a hot day, fill a <u>baby pool</u> with about an inch of water. Make sure the water is not too cold as you let baby sit in the pool and splash. Add some <u>toys that float and sink</u>. Let baby play with the toys while you watch him very closely.

Do you like playing in the water?
You are all wet!

Take baby out of the pool before he gets chilled or fussy. Dry him; cover him with a towel. Put him on a blanket in the sun.

 outdoors | 5–20 min | # 1–3 babies

246

Baby can

- reach for things on low shelves
- copy some movements

Patting Toy Animals

Have several soft cuddly <u>toy animals</u> on low shelves where baby can reach. When baby chooses an animal to play with, show her how to pat the animal.

Pat the puppy. Pat, pat, pat.
Can you pat the puppy?
Now can you pat the bear?

 indoors | 2–5 min | # 1–5 babies

247

Crawling in the Grass

Bring baby outside to a grassy, safe enclosed area where she can crawl and explore. As she stops to look at things, talk about what she sees, hears, or feels.

The grass is prickly. It tickles your hands, Anita.
Do you hear the bird? Tweet, tweet.
Listen. Hear the bird?

Make sure the area for crawling is safe. Remove anything that could harm baby and watch carefully.

Baby can

- understand some words

 outdoors | 5–20 min | # 1–6 babies

248

Cold Weather Clothes

When taking off <u>hats</u>, <u>coats</u>, and <u>mittens</u> after an outdoor walk or play-time, show baby how to help take things off. Help him reach up and pull off his hat. Talk about why he had these warm things on outside. Show him how happy you are as he helps.

It was so cold out, Cory! Your hat kept you warm.
Let's take it off now. Reach up. Grab your hat.
Good! You did it!

Baby can

- help pull off simple clothing

 indoors | 1–2 min | # 1 baby at a time

249

Smell the Flower

Bring <u>flowers</u> into the room and put them out of reach but where baby can see. Show baby the flowers and talk about them. Help baby touch flowers gently while you hold them. Put them near his nose so that he will smell them. Show him how you smell the flowers. Smell noisily so that he can hear you.

Smell the flower. It smells pretty.

Look at, touch, and smell flowers outside, too. Make sure baby doesn't try to eat the flowers; many flowers are poisonous.

Baby can

- see, hear, and smell things

 in or out | 2–5 min | # 1–6 babies

250

Baby can

- play peek-a-boo
- remember things not in view

Peek-A-Boo With Toy Animals

Show baby a <u>toy animal</u> and name it for him.

Here's a bear. Bear.

Hide the toy slowly behind your back and ask baby where it is. Quickly bring it back to where baby can see.

Here's the bear.

Play again if baby is interested.

 in or out | 2 – 10 min | # 1 – 5 babies

251

Baby can

- show interest in things farther away

Feeling Rain or Snow

On a day when it is very lightly raining or snowing, take baby out for a short walk. Dress baby warmly; don't take out a baby who is not feeling well. As you walk, talk about the rain or snow.

It's wet out here, isn't it?
There's a snowflake on your nose, Darla!
Is it cold?

When you come in, talk about how wet it was outside and how dry you are now.

 outdoors | 5 – 10 min | # 1 – 3 babies

252

Baby can

- place things into a container

Rocks and Containers

Put some <u>pretty</u>, <u>clean rocks</u> into a <u>plastic container</u>. Use a dishpan for the baby who is just learning to drop things into containers and a plastic wide-mouth bottle for the older baby. Make sure the rocks are big enough so that they won't be swallowed and small enough so that they can't hurt anyone. Help baby empty the container and then fill it again.

Can you drop the rock into the bowl?
That was a white one. And here's a gray one.

 in or out | 2 – 10 min | # 1 – 2 babies

Materials and Notes

Number

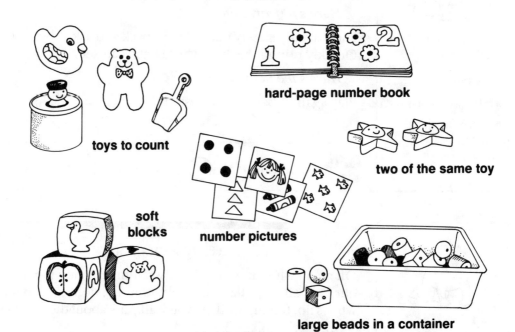

hard-page number book

toys to count

two of the same toy

soft blocks

number pictures

large beads in a container

- Counting with baby gives her a good beginning in understanding numbers. You can't expect baby to count for you, of course. That will come much later. But number skills can come more easily for a child who has often heard others counting.

- If baby is not interested in the counting you do, that is OK. Let baby play and learn in his own way.

- Make any counting you do with baby fun. Sing or chant numbers. Help baby pat or touch things as you count them.

- Explain to parents that counting with baby is important as she learns and stores away the skills she will need in school. Show them how counting can be fun and not a chore. Teach them a few counting songs they may not know.

Activity Checklist
Numbers

Number activities for infants include hearing an adult playfully count things, listening to number rhymes and songs, and hearing quantity and size words such as *one* and *many* or *big* and *little* used as part of everyday conversation. Number activities focus on introducing children to number ideas and words so that when they are older, counting and doing mathematics in school will come more easily.

Check for Each Age Group	*0–5 mo*	*5–9 mo*	*9–12 mo*
1. Colorful pictures and hard-page picture books showing a different numbers of familiar things are placed where child can see and touch them.	—	—	—
2. Adult sings or chants numbers, number songs, and number nursery rhymes to children during both routine care and play.	—	—	—
3. Adult often counts familiar things for child.	—	—	—
4. Adult uses quantity and size words for children when talking about familiar things the children can see.	—	—	—
5. Adult regularly looks at and talks about colorful number-picture books with children.			—

253

Look at Face Pictures

Make some <u>happy face pictures</u>. On one picture, put one big happy face, on another put two, and put eight or ten smaller faces on another. Hang one of these pictures where baby will be able to see it. Try putting it on the back of a rocking chair so that he will see it over your shoulder as you rock him.

See the picture. That's one face.
It has two eyes and one nose and one big smiling mouth.

Change the pictures often and talk about what baby sees.

Baby can

- see things 8″ – 12″ away

 in or out | 1 – 5 min | # 1 – 5 babies

254

Sing Number Songs

Make up little number songs and sing or chant them to baby whenever you can. Try one like this when baby is kicking her feet. Sing it to the tune of "Row, Row, Row Your Boat."

One, two, three, four, five
Kick your little feet.
One, two, three, four, five
In your infant seat.

Baby can

- kick legs actively
- sit supported

 in or out | 1 – 3 min | # 1 – 4 babies

255

Counting and Moving

Hold baby and sway back and forth or bend your knees to move up and down. Count to your rhythm as you move.

One, two, up, down. One, two, up, down.

Or put baby into a <u>carriage</u> or <u>stroller</u> and move it gently back and forth.

Back and forth, back and forth,
One, two, three, four.

Baby can

- enjoy being held

 in or out | 🕐 1 – 4 min | # 1 – 2 babies

256

Swinging and Singing

Put baby in a <u>baby swing</u> and start the swing moving gently back and forth. Sing or chant a number song to the rhythm of the swing. Try the rhyme "One, Two, Buckle My Shoe" or "One Little, Two Little, Three Little Babies." You will find the words to these on page 138.

Baby can

- sit supported

 in or out | 3–5 min | **#** 1 baby at a time

257

Toy Count

Put baby on her tummy on a soft <u>rug</u> or <u>blanket</u>. Have <u>a few toys</u> that you will give her one at a time.

Here are some toys for you, Eleanor.
Here's one, two, three!

Give her a toy as you say each number.

Three toys for you to play with.

Baby can

- lift head and chest while on stomach

 in or out | 1–2 min | **#** 1–6 babies

258

Bounces Count

Hold baby in a standing position so that he can bounce. As he bounces, count to five and then quickly lift baby up into the air.

One, two, three, four, five,
up you go!

If baby can't bounce by himself, help him by lifting him a little as you count, and then lift him high.

One, two, three, four! Five! Up you go!

Baby can

- bounce when held in a standing position

 in or out | 1–5 min | **#** 1 baby at a time

259

Baby can

- reach out to grab a toy

Counting Twos

While baby is sitting find two things to hand her to play with, such as <u>two teething toys or two big wooden spoons</u>. Attract her attention to the first toy and let her grab it. Then attract her attention to the second toy and give her that one, too.

Here's a big spoon. Do you want it?
Here's another. Take it.
Now you have two spoons. One, two.

Let baby play with the toys until she is ready for something new.

 in or out 1–2 min # 1 baby at a time

260

Baby can

- play with things by banging

Bang, Bang, Bang — One, Two, Three

Give baby <u>a toy that makes noise when he bangs it</u>. A big cooking spoon on a highchair tray will work well. Show him how to bang different number patterns.

Bang. I banged one time.
Bang bang bang. I banged three times.
One, two, three. That was three again.

Let baby use the toy to make noise in his own way. Count out loud with the hits he makes.

 in or out 2–10 min # 1–3 babies

261

Baby can

- put small things into mouth
- eat solid foods

How Many Little Pieces of Food?

While baby is waiting for lunch or if she is hungry and needs a tiny snack, put her into a highchair. Place three to six safe and easy-to-eat <u>small pieces of cereal</u> on the tray, one at a time. Count the cereal as you put each piece down.

Let baby pick up and eat the cereal. If you have time, count the pieces as she picks them up.

One, two, three.
You ate three Cheerios!

 indoors 1–10 min # 1–4 babies

262

Look at Pictures

Put together a collection of <u>large</u>, <u>brightly colored pictures</u>. Try to find pictures that have <u>different numbers of the same things</u>. Hang a few down low, where baby can see and touch them while playing. Cover the pictures with clear contact paper to keep them clean. Talk about the pictures as baby notices them.

See the puppies? One, two, three.
There are three puppies.

Change the pictures often.

 indoors 1–3 min **#** 1–6 babies

Baby can

- look at pictures

263

One Nose — Two Eyes

As you sit with babies who are playing, lift one or two who are not very busy onto your lap. Talk about how many eyes, noses, mouths, arms, legs, tummies, or fingers they have. Count their body parts, and tickle them gently. Get ready for any crawlers and toddlers in the area to join in the fun.

One little nose here, Tina.
And one little nose on you, Katy.
Two little noses!

Baby can

- show delight by cooing or smiling

 in or out 2–10 min **#** 1–6 babies

264

Rocking and Counting

When baby is having fun rocking back and forth on his hands and knees, join him in his game. Count as he rocks and chant your words with his rocking rhythm.

One, two, three, four,
Andy is rocking,
Back and forth.

Baby can

- rock when on hands and knees

 in or out ⊘ 1–2 min **#** 1 baby at a time

265

How Much Is in the Bottle?

As you cuddle baby while she is drinking from a <u>bottle</u>, talk about how much is in the bottle.

The bottle is full of milk now, Gina.
Now it's only half full.
It's almost empty. All gone!

Talk about how much when baby eats or drinks in other ways, too.

Baby can

- drink from a bottle

 in or out | 5 – 10 min | # 1 baby at a time

266

How Many Dropped?

Put baby in a <u>box</u> and prop him with <u>pillows</u> or put him in a <u>highchair</u>. Give him <u>toys</u> to play with while he sits. If he throws toys down out of reach, come over and talk about what he did.

You threw the toys down, Fred.
Where did they go? There they are!

As you pick up and return the toys to baby, count them for him.

Here's one, two, three! Now you can play again.

Baby can

- drop things
- look down for dropped things

 in or out | 1 – 5 min | # 1 – 6 babies

267

How Many Things in a Container?

Put five or six colorful <u>2″ beads</u> or <u>soft blocks</u> into a <u>dishpan</u>. Place the dishpan on a low shelf so that baby can reach it. Allow baby to pull out the dishpan and dump out the toys. Help her pick up the toys and drop them into the dishpan. Count the toys as she drops them in. Bring the dishpan and toys outside for baby to play with again. Use one dishpan for each baby.

You're putting the beads into the dishpan.
How many can you put in? One, two, three, four.

Baby can

- place things in a container

 in or out | 2 – 5 min | # 1 – 2 babies

268

Baby can

- pull up to stand but can't get down

1-2-3 Down You Go

Watch for baby who pulls up to stand and then can't get down. When she shows you she wants to sit, help her. As you help, talk about what she wants. Count to make getting down more fun.

Do you want to get down? I'll help you.
One, two, three. Down you go!

You can count when you help baby get down from her high-chair, crib, or the changing table, too.

 indoors | 1–2 min | # 1 baby at a time

269

Baby can

- look at pictures in books

Number Books

Place a few <u>hard-page number books</u> where baby can reach. When baby becomes interested, help him look at the pictures. Read what the book says if there are not too many words. Count the things in the pictures and point to each as you count.

If baby isn't interested in your reading or counting, try naming the things he sees instead.

 in or out | 1–10 min | # 1–4 babies

270

Baby can

- understand some words and directions

Toys to Count

Put <u>two of the same toys</u> on a low shelf where baby can reach. Sit near the shelf with baby. Ask her to hand you one of the toys.

Yoshi, where is the doll?
Give me the doll. Thank you.
Now give me the other doll. Thank you.

Count the toys with her as you point to each.

Now I have two dolls. One, two.

 indoors | 3–5 min | # 1–2 babies

271

Mealtime Counting

At mealtime, count for baby. Count the number of different things he has to eat, the number of spoonfuls he eats, or how many pieces of food there are.

Look, Adam. You have little pieces of cheese to eat.
1, 2, 3, 4, 5, 6. There are six pieces of cheese.
And four banana slices. 1, 2, 3, 4.
Can you feed yourself?

Baby can

- eat solid foods

 indoors | 1–2 min | # 1–6 babies

272

More Container Counting

Put about <u>ten 2″ blocks</u> into a <u>wide-mouth plastic jar</u> where baby can reach. Count as baby takes the blocks from the jar.

How many blocks are there, Juanita?
I'll count for you.

Try putting other safe things in the jar, such as clothespins, large wooden pegs, or big pop beads. Count these, too. If baby dumps all the things out at once count as you both put them back in.

Baby can

- explore things in a container

 in or out | 1–10 min | # 1 baby at a time

273

Blocks Count

Show baby how to put one plastic or foam block on top of another. Count as you stack the blocks.

One block, two blocks.
Look, I put one block on top of the other.

Let baby try to stack. Count the blocks as she tries.

Baby can

- stack one toy on top of another

 indoors | 3–5 min | # 1–3 babies

274

How Many Babies?

When babies are ready for lunch or a walk, gently touch and count each baby. Chant a little rhyme as you do so.

One baby, two babies, three babies, and me.
Let's go on a walk and see what we'll see.
Two in the stroller and one in the pack.
First we'll go out and then we'll come back.

Baby can

- enjoy rhymes

 in or out | 1–2 min | # 1–3 babies

275

Count and Dress

As you help baby get dressed, playfully touch each finger or toe and count to her.

Here are your fingers.
One, two, three, four, five.
Five little fingers on your hand.

Play other counting games as you dress baby. Count her other body parts, clothes, or diapers.

Baby can

- understand some words

 in or out | 1–2 min | # 1 baby at a time

276

Nesting Toy Count

Put <u>several sets of nesting toys</u> on a low shelf. Try plastic measuring cups or mixing bowls of different sizes that all fit into each other. When baby takes a set from the shelf and pulls them apart, talk about the number of parts that fit together.

There were lots of smaller bowls in that big one.
One, two, three, four.
Four bowls to play with, Maria.
Oh! You put the little one into the bigger one.

Baby can

- fit one thing into another

 in or out | 1–6 min | # 1–2 babies

Activities for Learning from the World Around Them

Materials and Notes
Five Senses

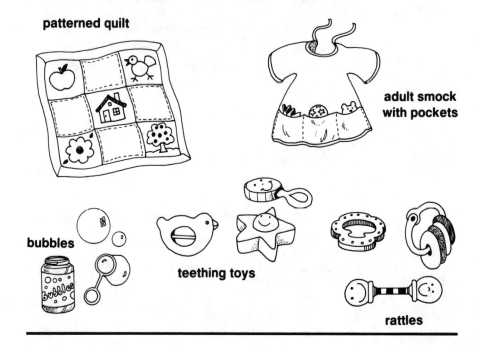

patterned quilt

adult smock with pockets

bubbles

teething toys

rattles

- Baby uses all her senses — seeing, hearing, touching, smelling, and especially tasting — to find out about her world. It is natural for baby to put everything she can pick up into her mouth.

- Remember to add talking to everything baby sees, feels, tastes, hears, or smells. This will help baby learn to talk.

- Make sure that anything baby can reach or touch is safe and clean. Check buttons or small pieces to see that they are secure. Pay special attention when string toys or balloons are used. Make sure nothing baby touches could cause cuts, bumps, choking, poisoning, or any other harm.

- Help parents with ideas for making sure baby is safe while free to explore and learn at home.

Activity Checklist

Five Senses

For infants and toddlers, using the five senses is the most natural way to learn. Babies enjoy tasting and feeling things in their mouths to learn. Toddlers continue to do this, but their other senses are used more as they reach two years of age. Activities for infants help them become familiar with words that describe what they sense and give them experiences in using their senses in many different, enjoyable ways.

Check for Each Age Group	*0–5 mo*	*5–9 mo*	*9–12 mo*
1. Soft areas are provided in the environment: cuddly toys, cushions, soft rugs.	—	—	—
2. Indoor noise level is generally low and comfortable; unnecessary background noise is avoided (record player is turned off when short music time is over).	—	—	—
3. Pictures, mobiles, and other objects are placed where they are easy for children to see (near cribs, highchairs, and diapering area; low on walls and furniture).	—	—	—
4. Toys of different colors, shapes, textures, or sound qualities are accessible to children daily.	—	—	—
5. Adult talks with child about what the child is sensing (talks with child about taste and smell of food; points out colors and shapes of toys child uses).	—	—	—
6. Foods served to children have little or no added salt or sugar and are not heavily spiced so that children can enjoy natural flavors and smells.	—	—	

277

Baby can

- look at pictures

Pattern Pictures

Draw <u>pattern pictures</u> for baby to look at. Try checker boards, spirals, snowflakes, crossed lines, or make up some of your own. The patterns should be different sizes on <u>paper that is 5″ or larger</u> and drawn with <u>wide-tip</u>, <u>colorful markers</u>. Put these pictures up all around the room where baby can easily see them.

Change baby's position often so that she won't get bored with looking at the same thing.

 in or out | 1–2 min | # 1–6 babies

278

Baby can

- look in a mirror

See the Baby

Put up a large <u>unbreakable mirror</u> beside the changing table. Point to baby in the mirror while you are diapering and talk about what you see.

Oh look! See the baby. That's you, Desmond!
You are having your diaper changed.

Pick baby up so that he can see himself better when you are finished changing.

 indoors | 1–5 min | # 1 baby at a time

279

Baby can

- hear sounds

Jingling Sounds

Make a mobile by hanging a couple of <u>bells</u> or <u>rattles</u> from a <u>coat hanger or wooden dowel</u>. Hang the mobile near baby in an <u>infant seat</u> or play area. Use one mobile for one or two babies. Move the things on the mobile or hang them in the wind so that baby can listen to the sounds they make.

Listen. Do you hear that jingle?
It's a bell ringing in the wind.

 in or out | 3–5 min | # 1–4 babies

280

Talking With Baby

Talk to baby using lots of different pitches in your voice. Try whispering, high and low soft sounds, singing your words, little squeaks and squeals, or other sounds that baby likes to hear. Don't use very loud sounds that might scare baby.

Listen. I'm whispering your name.
I love you, Rachel.

Baby can
- hear sounds

 in or out | 1–10 min | # 1–5 babies

281

Find the Sound

Gently shake a <u>bell</u> or <u>rattle</u> over baby's head. Then move it to the side of his head and shake it again. See if baby will turn his head to find the sound. Shake the rattle on baby's other side and see if he will turn to see where the sound comes from. Slowly move the rattle around his head and watch him find the sounds.

Listen! Can you find that rattle?

Baby can
- hear sounds

 in or out | 1–10 min | # 1–2 babies

282

Smells in the Room

Talk with baby about the smells in the room: a teacher's new perfume, the toddler's food, sweet smelling powder, flower smells in an outdoor breeze. Breathe deeply through your nose for baby to watch as you talk.

Mmm, smell those potatoes.
Don't they smell good?

Baby can
- smell foods

 indoors | 2–15 min | # 1–6 babies

Activities for Learning from the World Around Them

283

Smell the Vanilla

Put a little bit of <u>vanilla extract</u> on your hand or neck. Hold baby where she can be near the smell and talk with her about it.

> *Mmm. Do you smell that, Patricia?*
> *That smells good doesn't it? It's vanilla.*

Don't try this with strong perfumes; baby may not like a strong smell.

Baby can

- smell things around her

 in or out | 2 – 10 min | # 1 – 2 babies

284

Feelie Blankets

Place baby on <u>big cloths of different textures</u>. Try this when baby is wearing only a diaper as well as at times when he is fully dressed. Use textures such as fleece; soft, fuzzy fabrics; smooth, slippery satin; nubby towels; soft, cuddly, old sweaters. Tell baby about what he is feeling.

> *Doesn't that feel nice? It's so soft.*

Try this as an outdoor activity on a nice, sunny day.

Baby can

- feel the things around him

 in or out | 2 – 10 min | # 1 – 6 babies

285

Animal Rub

Find <u>stuffed animals</u> made from different kinds of material. Rub the animals on different parts of baby's body so that he can feel how soft and cuddly they are. Leave these toys out for baby to play with, watch, and feel.

> *That's the kitten on your tummy, Benny.*
> *Doesn't that feel good?*

Baby can

- feel the things around him

 in or out | 1 – 10 min | # 1 – 6 babies

Activities for Learning from the World Around Them

286

Blowing on Baby

Take baby's hand and blow gently onto her palm.

I'm blowing on your hand.
Can you feel that?

Blow on other parts of baby and tell her what you are doing.

I'm going to get your toes.
Can you feel that?

Baby can

- feel the things
  around her

 in or out | 2–10 min | **#** 1–2 babies

287

Textured Teethers

Give each baby a <u>teething toy</u> that feels and looks different. Try ones with bumps and ridges on them or others that are smooth. Tell baby what she is feeling.

Oh, doesn't that feel good in your mouth, Linda?
It's bumpy.

Be sure to clean teething toys when a baby has finished with them.

Baby can

- mouth things

 in or out | 2–10 min | **#** 1–6 babies

288

Mouthing Your Finger

Wave your fingers in front of baby so that she can watch them move. See if she will reach out and grab your finger. As she holds on, let her pull your fingers to her mouth so that she can teethe on them. Try rubbing her gums so that she can feel your touch. Baby may often be comforted by just sucking on the side of your finger.

Note: Thoroughly wash your hands with soap and water before and after this activity.

Baby can

- mouth things

 in or out | 1–10 min | **#** 1 baby at a time

289

Mirrors on the Floor

Lay a large, sturdy, <u>unbreakable mirror</u> flat on the floor. Put baby on the mirror and show him his reflection. Talk with baby about what he sees.

Oh, look. There you are, Mañuel.
See your red shirt?

Baby can

- push up
- sit unsupported

 in or out | 2–10 min | # 1–4 babies

290

Dancing Sunlight

Sit with baby on the floor on a bright, sunny day. Show her how the sunlight shines on the floor. Wave your hand over the light to make shadows move in the sun. Tell baby about that she sees.

Oh look, Marcia. See the sunlight!
Watch my fingers dance.

Try this activity outside on a blanket or under a tree.

Baby can

- watch moving things

 in or out | 2–15 min | # 1–6 babies

291

Colored Windows

Put several pieces of <u>colored cellophane</u> up on the window. Take baby over to the windows and show her the pretty colors that shine through. While baby is playing on the floor or in other areas of the room, point out the colored spots that shine through onto the rug or the toys.

Look, Leigh. Look at the pretty colors.

Baby can

- look at colorful things

 indoors | 1–5 min | # 1–6 babies

292

Colored Rooms

Put a <u>colored lightbulb</u> in one of the lights in your room. Talk with baby about the new colors she sees.

Rosa, see the shiny green light?
It makes your shirt look green, too.

Baby can

- look at colorful things

 indoors | 1–3 min | **#** 1–6 babies

293

Find the Toy

While baby is sitting on the floor, choose a <u>colorful jingling toy</u> and shake it in front of him. When you are sure he is watching, move the toy slowly from one side to the other. Help baby turn his body to follow the toy and watch it wherever it goes.

Find the bear, Julio.
Look around. It's over here.

Baby can

- watch moving things

 in or out | 2–7 min | **#** 1–3 babies

294

Crumple the Paper

Sit with baby on the floor and noisily crumple a piece of clean <u>newsprint</u> or <u>giftwrap</u>.

What a loud noise! Can you make one, too?

Help baby crumple his own paper and make his own crumpling noise. Try tossing a piece of paper down on the floor or over to the side. See if baby hears the noise of the dropped paper and looks around to find it.

Baby can

- listen to sounds
- watch moving things

 in or out | 2–10 min | **#** 1–6 babies

295

Where Am I?

Call to baby from different places in the room. Talk to him and tell him what you are doing. Move to another area of the room and call again to baby. Help him to find your voice wherever you move.

Hey, Thomas! I'm over here changing Melissa.
Can you find me?

Baby can
- look for sounds

 in or out 2–7 min **#** 1–6 babies

296

Tick Tock Goes the Clock

Bring in a loud <u>ticking</u> wind-up <u>clock</u>. Show it to baby and move it close to her ear so that she can hear the sounds it makes.

Hear it tick? Tick tock, tick tock.
Tick tock goes the clock.

Baby can
- listen to sounds

 in or out 1–5 min **#** 1–4 babies

297

Smelly Bottles

Poke several small holes in the lids of <u>empty plastic bottles</u>. Put two or three <u>cotton balls</u> into each bottle. Then sprinkle a different <u>spice</u>, such as cinnamon, allspice, cloves, or vanilla or peppermint extract onto the cotton balls. Securely fasten the lids. Give the smelly bottles to baby to smell and play with.

Oh, that smells nice doesn't it, Alicia.
It smells like cinnamon.

Baby can
- grasp toys
- smell things

 in or out 2–10 min **#** 1–2 babies

298

Baby can

- eat solid foods

Smelling Food

At feeding time, talk with baby about the smells of food.

Mmm. I smell green beans.
Tara, you have green beans.

Name all the different foods that baby is smelling as she eats.

 in or out | 2–10 min | # 1–6 babies

299

Baby can

- hear sounds
- feel and see things around him

What's Outside?

Take baby outside for a walk or to play on a big <u>blanket</u>. Talk with him about the things he can smell or hear outside. Bring things for him to touch, see, and smell from a garden or nearby bush. Show him the pretty leaves rustling in the trees and how their shadows move on the ground. Listen for birds, cars, or other outdoor noises and tell baby all about them.

 outdoors | 2–20 min | # 1–6 babies

300

Baby can

- feel the things around her

Feelie Smock

Make a feelie smock from an <u>old shirt or apron</u>. Sew <u>different textured scraps of materials</u> all over the shirt. Stuff scraps of material in the pockets and leave pieces of the fabric sticking out for baby to grab. Wear this feelie smock while you are caring for baby. Encourage her to find, rub, touch, and play with all the new textures she finds.

Look, Greta. See the pink fuzz?
It's so soft!

 in or out | 2–10 min | # 1–6 babies

301

Baby can

- hold his bottle

Bottle Cover

Cover baby's <u>bottle</u> with a textured material, such as a <u>nubby washcloth</u>, <u>slippery stocking</u> or <u>fuzzy sock</u>. Give it to baby to hold onto as you cuddle and feed her.

You have a fuzzy bottle.
You are feeling it while you drink.

 in or out   2–10 min   # 1 baby at a time

302

Baby can

- feel the things around her

Body Parts

Help baby use her hand to touch your hair. Tell her what she is doing and describe for her how it feels.

That's my hair, Callie.
It's long and soft.
See, it goes down to my shoulders.

After she touches your hair, have her touch her own hair. Go back and forth touching different body parts, naming each one and saying what each one feels like.

 in or out   2–10 min   # 1–4 babies

303

Baby can

- feed himself finger foods

Tasting Treats

After baby has started eating <u>solid foods and finger foods</u> try having little tasting parties at mealtimes or snacks. Give baby lots of different things to taste and tell him about what he is eating: a hard Cheerio or soft piece of peach, a mild piece of banana or tart orange juice, a warm cooked green bean or a cold cheese cube.

That cheese is cold, Michael.
Doesn't it taste good?

 in or out   2–15 min   # 1–6 babies

304

Baby can

- watch your mouth
- begin to copy a few sounds

Feel and Say a Sound

Sit in front of baby where he can easily see your face. Make a sound over and over that you know baby enjoys making. Try putting baby's hand on your mouth so that he can feel your lips move as well as see them. See if he will copy you or even move his mouth as he tries to do what you do.

Ba, ba, ba, ba, ba!
Good, Casey! That's right.
Your mouth can move just like mine.

 in or out   2–7 min   # 1–4 babies

305

Baby can

- watch moving things

Bubbles

Sit with baby in an open area. Gently blow a <u>soap bubble</u> in front of him where he can easily watch it float through the air.

Look Rick! See the bubble?
Watch it float in the air.

After baby can follow a big bubble right in front of him, blow the bubble a little harder so that baby can watch it float away.

 in or out   2–10 min   # 1–6 babies

306

Baby can

- look at pictures

Children's Picture Book

Take some <u>pictures of the children in your room</u> or ask parents to send in a picture they no longer want. Cover these pictures with <u>clear contact paper</u> and punch 1 or 2 holes in the side of each picture. Tie all of them together with <u>yarn or string</u> to make your Children's Picture Book.

Oh look, Melika! There you are!
You're sitting on your daddy's lap.

 in or out   2–10 min   # 1–6 babies

307

Baby can

- watch moving things

Watch the Balloon

Hang some brightly colored <u>balloons</u> out of reach but where baby can see them. Put them in a place where there is a breeze so that the balloons bounce around. As baby watches the balloons, tell him about what he sees.

That's a red balloon, Timmy. See it fly?

Note: Do *not* let baby play with balloons. Pick up broken balloon pieces and throw them away immediately. When helium balloons lose helium, tie them out of reach.

 in or out | 2–10 min | # 1–6 babies

308

Baby can

- turn to find sounds

Finding Different Sounds

Put three different <u>sound-making toys</u> such as bells, a spoon and pot, a drum, or a rattle on different corners of a big blanket. While baby is sitting on the blanket make one of the sounds for her to hear, find, and crawl to.

Here it is, Tammy. Jingle, jingle goes the bell.

Move to another corner of the blanket and make another sound for baby. Try the activity once each day for a few days. See if baby gets better at finding the new sounds.

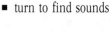 in or out | 2–10 min | # 1–6 babies

309

Baby can

- watch you
- try to copy sounds

Making Noises With Baby

Sit with baby so that she can see your face. Stick your tongue out at her and make a funny face. Try to make baby laugh and copy your funny noise. If other babies are nearby but not looking at you, make the noise again to see if they will turn and find you.

I made a funny noise, didn't I.
Did you like that?

in or out | 2–7 min | # 1–6 babies

Activities for Learning from the World Around Them

310

What Do You Hear?

Make a <u>tape of the familiar sounds</u> baby hears, such as water running, toilet flushing, clock ticking, or toys banging. Sit with baby and play the tape. Name the sound she hears and point to the things that make the noise she hears.

Lucy, do you hear that?
That's a telephone. Ring, ring.
Where's the telephone in our room?
Here it is!

Baby can

- listen to familiar sounds

 indoors | 2–7 min | # 1–4 babies

311

After the Rain

Take baby outside after a fresh rain and talk about all the new smells. Touch cool water on soft flower petals or watch the rain make a stream as it flows away. Smell the air filled with moisture. Talk with baby about what you smell, see, and feel.

Touch the flower, Amanda.
It's wet, isn't it?

Baby can

- smell, touch and look at the things around her

 outdoors | 2–10 min | # 1–4 babies

312

Books of Smells

Read <u>picture books that have scratch and smell places on the pages</u>. Talk about the pictures and scratch the sniffing places for baby to smell.

See the pink flower, Teddie? It's a rose.
Doesn't it smell pretty?

Baby can

- smell things
- look at books

 in or out | 2–10 min | # 1–3 babies

Activities for Learning from the World Around Them

313

Mobiles to Smell

Cut out a few 6″ circles of <u>brightly colored material</u>. Put a few drops of <u>vanilla</u>, <u>lemon</u>, <u>or almond extract</u> onto <u>cotton balls</u> and securely tie these up in your material with <u>string or yarn</u>. Tie <u>some cloves</u> or <u>potpourri</u> in other pieces of material. Securely hang several of these smelling bags from a <u>hanger or dowel</u> where baby can see and just manage to hit them. Watch her face as new smells fill her play spacc. Talk about them for her.

I smell vanilla, Margaret. Do you?

Baby can

- hit at moving things

 indoors | 2 – 10 min | # 1 – 2 babies

314

Warm and Cold

Give baby <u>things of different temperatures</u> to play with. Freeze water in empty butter tubs. Then put the piece of ice on an <u>old rug square</u> for baby to touch and move. Or float the ice in warm water for baby to play with. Lay baby's toys in a sunny window so that they will feel warm when he goes to play with them.

Oh! That ice is cold!

Watch baby carefully if he is playing with ice. Remove ice that has melted so that baby doesn't choke on small pieces.

Baby can

- feel the things around him

 in or out | 2 – 10 min | # 1 – 6 babies

315

Swing Through the Air

Pick up baby, supporting her firmly around her middle. Swing her gently through the air. Talk to her about where she is and how it feels.

You're up so high, Sandy! Is that fun?
Can you feel the wind in your face?

Try this activity other times in other ways. Swing with baby in your lap or talk to baby while she's in a baby swing in the room.

Baby can

- feel the wind moving around her

 in or out | 2 – 7 min | # 1 baby at a time

316

Baby can

- crawl around the room

Textured Rug Squares

Lay <u>rug squares</u> of different colors and textures out across the room. Put them in the places where baby most often crawls and let him explore the area.

You're on the red rug, Ned. It feels so smooth.
See Dora? She is on the bumpy, green square.

Try this activity outside, too.

 in or out | 2–15 min | # 1–6 babies

317

Baby can

- feel things of different texture

Tickle Time

Gently tickle baby on different parts of his body and tell him what you are doing.

I'm going to get your tummy, Ken.
Tickle, tickle. I got you!

Try tickling baby with things that feel different, such as a feather, a stuffed animal, your hair, or a fuzzy cloth.

 in or out | 2–7 min | # 1–4 babies

318

Baby can

- move to explore

Texture Boxes

Find a <u>box</u> big enough for a baby to crawl around in. Line the boxes with <u>materials of different textures</u> so that when baby plays in the box she can touch the box sides and feel the material.

Ann is touching the yellow felt.
See how soft it is?

 in or out | 2–7 min | # 1–2 babies

319

Tasting Different Textures

Give baby <u>foods of different textures</u> to taste and feel. Tell him about what he is eating.

You're eating a hard cracker.
Crunch, crunch, crunch goes the cracker.

Try soft peaches, applesauce, or oatmeal; crunchy crackers, cereal, or toast.

Note: Be sure type and amount of food is safe for baby. Some babies eat and chew better than others.

Baby can
- eat solid foods

 in or out | 2–10 min | **#** 1–6 babies

320

Dishpan Teething Toys

Put an <u>assortment of toys</u> that are safe for baby to chew on in a <u>dishpan</u>. Get several different textures. Put the dishpan of teething toys out for baby to play with. Tell her what she feels.

That's a hard block. Feel the edge?

Try things such as new plastic dish scrubbers, big round rattles, a frisbee, stacking rings, or toy cups.

Note: Make sure toys are kept clean and safe.

Baby can
- chew on toys

 in or out | 5–15 min | **#** 1–6 babies

321

Refrigerated Toys

Put baby's pacifier, teethers, or other <u>mouthing toys</u> in the <u>refrigerator</u> to get cold. Give each baby her own toys to chew on and talk about their cold feeling.

Oh! Latarsha, that's cold, isn't it?
It's been in the refrigerator.

Baby can
- chew on toys

 in or out | 2–10 min | **#** 1–6 babies

322

Words With Actions

Do special actions with the words you say often to baby. For example, put your hands up over your head when you ask baby if she wants to be picked up. Or put your hands to your lips when you tell baby it's time to eat. See if baby will do the actions with you once she's seen them with the words many times.

Up, Janet? Do you want me to pick you up?
You put up your hands.
I know you want to get up.

Baby can

- understand some words
- copy some actions

 in or out | 1–2 min | # 1–2 babies

323

Upside-Down World

Sit in a <u>sturdy chair</u> and stretch out your legs. Have baby sit on your lap, facing you. Gently lay him down on his back along your outstretched legs so he's a little bit upside-down. Talk about the things he can see.

What do you see, Joshua? Do you see the highchair? It's upside-down.

Then gently pull him up and turn him so he can see the same things right-side up.

Baby can

- understand some familiar words

 in or out | 1–2 min | # 1 baby at a time

324

Foot Play

Have baby lie on your lap, on her back, with her head at your knees. Then play with her feet to let her feel what they can do. Rub the soles of her feet together. Clap them together, too. Gently see if baby can touch her toes to her chin or nose. Wiggle each of her toes. You can sing to baby as you move her feet.

I've got your little feet!
They can clap, clap, clap.
They can go up and down, up and down.

Baby can

- enjoy some gentle active play

 in or out | 2–5 min | # 1 baby at a time

Materials and Notes

Shape, Size, and Color

soft dolls

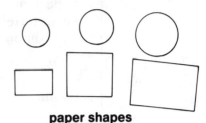

paper shapes

stacking rings

shape cans

bottles to shake

- Give baby experiences with things of different shapes, sizes, and colors. He will store up what he learns.
- When putting up mobiles or pictures for baby to look at, make sure you put them where baby tends to look most often.
- Watch carefully when using strings, toys with small pieces, heavy toys, or anything else that might harm baby. Use these when other babies are sleeping or safely involved in another activity. Put them away when done.
- Help parents with ideas for talking about shape, size, or color with baby. Some ideas to give them are talking about color of clothes, shapes of toys, and size of people or animals.

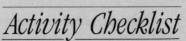

Activity Checklist

Shape, Size, and Color

Shape, size and color activities for infants include activities in which an adult points out those attributes while the child experiences and explores toys, pictures, and other familiar things. The child becomes familiar with the words that describe shape, size, and color from repeated experiences in hearing the words while playing with objects.

Check for Each Age Group	*0 – 5 mo*	*5 – 9 mo*	*9 – 12 mo*
1. Chances to explore things with obvious variety in shape, size and color are offered daily in play.	—	—	—
2. Adult often points out and talks to children about the shape, size, and color of toys and other familiar things the child sees during both play and routine care.	—	—	—
3. Pictures and mobiles that show a variety of shapes, sizes, and colors are put where child can easily see them.	—	—	—

325

Rocking Chair Pictures

Put <u>shape pictures</u> of different sizes and colors on the back of a <u>rocking chair</u>. When you hold baby, put her up on your shoulder where she can easily see the colors and shapes.

Look, Micki. See the circle? It's red.
You can touch it if you want to.

Change the pictures often to keep baby interested.

Baby can

- look at things

 indoors | 2–10 min | # 1 baby at a time

326

Big Ball, Little Ball

Find several <u>balls</u> of different sizes or colors. While baby is lying on her back, roll one of the balls across her tummy. Tell her about it as you move it over her body.

Feel the ball, Cathy. It's round and big.

Roll another ball and give it to baby to hold and look at. Try to use balls that are light and colorful, such as beach balls.

Baby can

- move arms and legs in play

 in or out | 1–4 min | # 1–3 babies

327

Color and Size Mobiles

Make a mobile of similar <u>things that are different colors or sizes</u>, such as soft blocks, faces drawn on different colored paper, or rattles. Hang it in a place where baby can easily see and hit it. As baby plays with the mobile, talk with her about what she's doing. Use one mobile for each baby.

See the big block? It's green and soft.
You hit it!

Baby can

- hit at things

 in or out | 2–10 min | # 1–2 babies

328

Feel the Toy

Find <u>easy-to-hold toys that are the same shape but of different sizes or textures</u>. Give baby one toy and let her play with it while you hold the second toy where she can easily see it. Then trade with her and let her hold the second toy. Talk with her about the things she sees and feels.

That's a fuzzy bear, Megan.
It is soft. Now hold this one.
It's plastic. It feels hard and smooth.

Baby can

■ begin to hold toys

 in or out | 1–4 min | # 1–3 babies

329

Color and Shape Cuffs

Cut off the <u>cuff of a baby's sock</u> to make a small ring of fabric. Securely sew small <u>colored pieces of material</u> onto the cuffs. Make several at one time and use material of different textures to make different size and color shapes on the cuff. Slip one of these over baby's ankle or wrist and help him look at it.

Look, Juan. This is a red square.
Can you see it?

Baby can

■ look at his hands and feet

 in or out | 1–10 min | # 1–4 babies

330

Bang the Blocks

Have baby sit in his highchair. Give him two <u>blocks of different sizes</u>, <u>weights</u>, <u>or textures</u> to bang on his tray. Talk with him about what he is doing.

Bang. Bang. That one makes a big noise.
Now try another one. What sound does it make?

Talk about the different sounds or sizes of the blocks. Be sure to take baby out of his highchair as soon as he is done playing.

Baby can

■ bang things on a tray

 indoors | 3–5 min | # 1–6 babies

Activities for Learning from the World Around Them

331

Pull the Strings

Put <u>toys of different sizes and weights</u> on the ends of several <u>strings</u>. Lay one of the strings out in front of where baby is sitting. Show her how to pull it so that the toy moves toward her. Give her the string to pull and talk with her about what she is doing.

Pull the string, Carmen. It's heavy, isn't it?

Let her try pulling another toy to feel the difference in weight.

Baby can

- pull a string

 in or out | 2–5 min | # 1 baby at a time

332

Shake the Bottles

Find two or three easy-to-hold <u>plastic bottles</u>. Fill them with different amounts of <u>beans</u> and securely attach each lid. <u>Glue or tape</u> the lid on tightly. Give each baby two or three bottles to shake, and talk about their sound, weight, and movement.

Shake, shake, shake.
Oh. That's a loud noise.
What a heavy bottle.

Baby can

- shake a small bottle

 in or out | 1–10 min | # 1–2 babies

333

Dropping Toys

Find a <u>can or metal bowl</u> that will make a good noise if something drops in it. Add several <u>toys or blocks</u> of different shapes, sizes, and textures. Hold one toy over the can and drop it while baby watches you. Talk about the size of the toy, what shape it is, and the sound it makes. Give baby a toy to drop on her own.

Listen. That's a big noise!
Here, try another toy.
What sound does it make?

Baby can

- drop things on purpose

 in or out | 3–5 min | # 1–4 babies

334

Textured Shapes

Glue <u>textured materials</u> to <u>cardboard squares</u>, <u>circles</u>, <u>and triangles of different sizes</u>. Make sure you have both a big shape and little shape of each material. While baby is sitting in his highchair, give him one or two pairs of the shapes. Tell him about them while he plays.

You have two red squares.
One is big and the other is little.
They feel soft.

Baby can

- grasp things

 indoors | 2–10 min | # 1–3 babies

335

Peek-A-Boo With Colors and Shapes

Cut out <u>different brightly colored paper or cloth shapes</u>. Hold one in front of your face and play peek-a-boo with baby. Tell him all about the color or shape you are hiding behind. Try covering baby with the cloth or putting the paper over his face for just a few seconds. Play peek-a-boo that way, too.

Where's Damon? Peek-a-boo!
You were behind the blue triangle!

Baby can

- play peek-a-boo

 in or out | 1–10 min | # 1–3 babies

336

Finding Colors

Find two or three <u>similar toys that are different colors</u>, such as a red, a blue, and a green block. Hide them, one at a time, under a <u>white cloth</u> as baby watches. Let baby try to uncover the blocks herself. As she uncovers them, talk with her about the color and size of each.

Look, Liza. You found a green block.
It's a square.

Baby can

- uncover hidden things

 in or out | 2–7 min | # 1–3 babies

337

Feelie Shapes

Glue <u>colored or textured material</u> to 3″ <u>cardboard</u> shapes. Give these shapes to baby to play with and rub. Talk with her about how they feel or look.

Feel the circle, Cindy.
Make your finger go round and round.

Baby can

- poke with a pointing finger

 in or out | 2–10 min | # 1–4 babies

338

Feelie Boxes

Glue <u>textured materials</u> to the inside of <u>small boxes</u>, such as tissue boxes or shoe boxes. Cut a big enough hole for baby's hand in one end of the box and tape the lid back on. Give the box to baby so that he can feel and explore how the inside of the box feels.

Put your hand in here.
It feels slippery.

Baby can

- explore with fingers and hands

 in or out | 1–10 min | # 1–6 babies

339

Roll the Balls

Find several <u>balls of different sizes and weights</u>. Roll one to baby and help her to roll it back.

Roll it to me. That's a big ball.
It's not very heavy, though.
It's a beach ball.

Try rolling another ball of a different size. Talk with baby about how it is different and what it looks like.

Baby can

- try to roll a ball

 in or out | 2–10 min | # 1–4 babies

340

A Truck Full of Blocks

Help baby roll a <u>light plastic dumptruck</u> back and forth a few times. Then put several <u>blocks</u> in the back of the truck to make it heavier to push.

Oh. That truck is getting heavy.
It's harder to push.

Try adding more and more blocks to help baby feel different weights.

Baby can

■ try to roll a truck

 in or out | 2–10 min | # 1–3 babies

341

Nesting Cups

Find two or three <u>bowls</u> or <u>boxes</u> that <u>fit inside of each other</u>, such as nesting blocks, mixing bowls, or butter tubs. Give baby the smallest bowl and show her how to put it in the larger one.

Put it in, Shirley.
It's little, so it will fit into the big one.

After she can nest two cups successfully, give her one more so that she can nest three cups.

Baby can

■ put one thing inside another

 in or out | 1–10 min | # 1–2 babies

342

Dropping Blocks in a Cup

Use a <u>plastic container and several different sizes of blocks</u>, some that fit in the container and some that don't. Use only blocks that are too big for baby to choke on. Play a game with baby to drop the blocks in the container one at a time.

Look. That one went in. It's a little block.
Oh, no. This block is too big. It won't fit.

Baby can

■ drop things on purpose

 in or out | 2–10 min | # 1–4 babies

343

Stacking Things

Use <u>stacking rings or several different sized blocks</u>. Put one ring or block down in front of baby and stack another on top as he watches. Give baby one to stack. Talk with him about what he is doing.

Oh, Clay. That fits on top. It's a little blue ring.

Baby can

- put one thing on top of another

 in or out | 2–10 min | # 1–4 babies

344

Shape Cans

Cut a circle or a square in the <u>plastic lid</u> of a <u>coffee can</u>. Make sure the shape is big enough for round or square blocks to fit through easily. Push a block down into the hole as baby watches. Tell him what you are doing. Then give him a block to put into the can. Watch to see if he will copy what you did. Then let baby play with the blocks and coffee can in his own way.

Did you hear the block hit the bottom of the can?

Be sure the can has no rough edges or use a plastic container.

Baby can

- drop things into a small opening

 in or out | 1–10 min | # 1–2 babies

345

Touch and Feel Books

Cover square 6″ pieces of <u>cardboard with different textured materials</u>. Punch two holes along one edge of each piece and tie them all together to make a book. Let baby play with the book as you talk about what he feels.

That's a blue page. See how fluffy it is.

Try making some shapes out of contrasting materials and sewing them on top of a few pages for baby to feel and touch.

Baby can

- turn pages in a hard-page book

 in or out | 3–10 min | # 1–4 babies

Your Own Activities for Learning from the World Around Them

Write your own activities on these three pages. You will find more information on writing your own activities in the Planning section, pages 12–13.

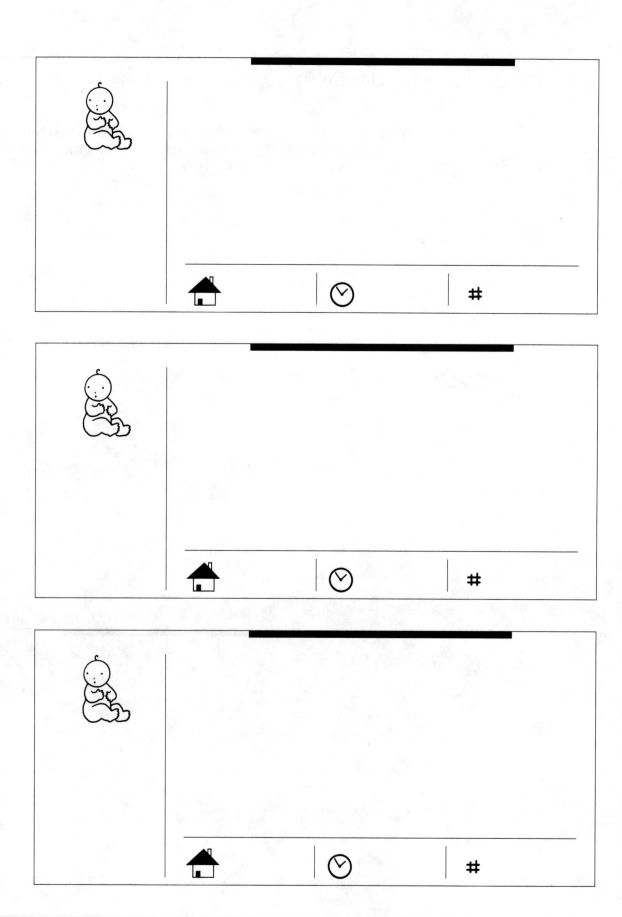

Activities for Learning from the World Around Them

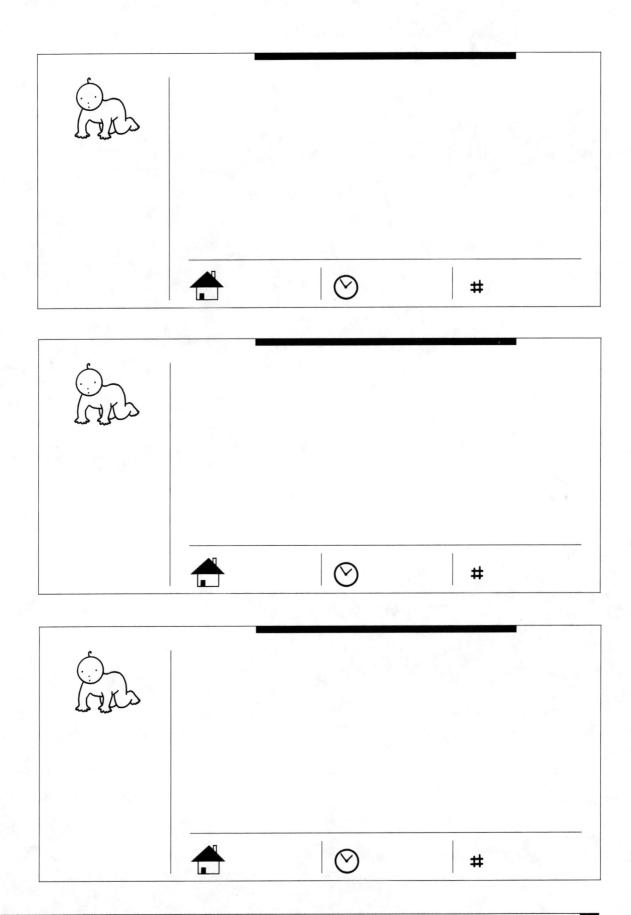